The Ultimate Pop Sheet Music Collection 2000

D0800512

Contents

ALL MY LIFE

Words and Music by
RORY BENNETT and
JO JO HAILEY

All My Life - 7 - 1

Verse:

1. I will nev-er find an-oth-er lov-er sweet-er than you, sweet-er than you.___ And

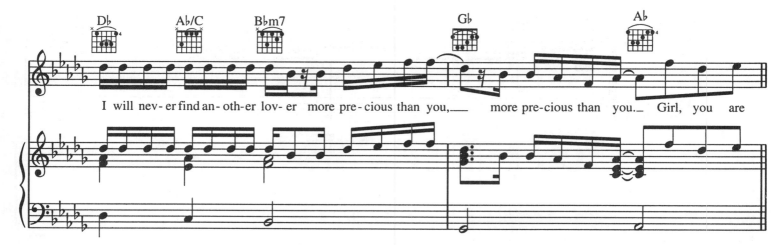

I will nev-er find an-oth-er lov-er more pre-cious than you,___ more pre-cious than you.___ Girl, you are

close to me, you're like my moth-er; close to me, you're like my fa-ther; close to me, you're like my sis-ter; close to me, you're like my broth-er.
2. *See additional lyrics*

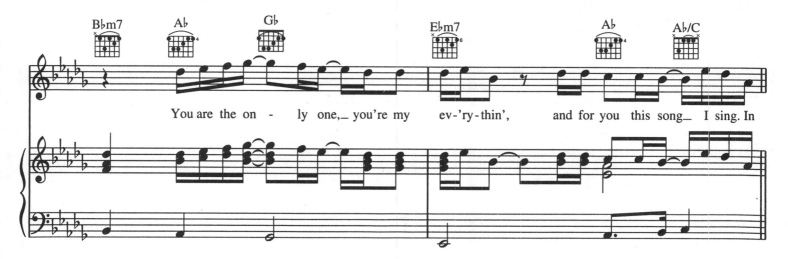

You are the on - ly one,___ you're my ev-'ry-thin',___ and for you this song___ I sing. In

6

Chorus:

all my life, _____ I pray for some-one___ like you. And

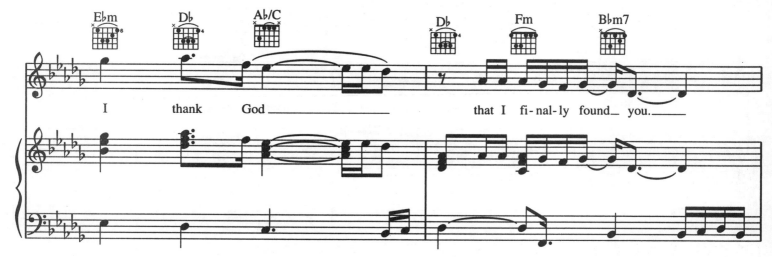

I thank God _____ that I fi-nal-ly found___ you._____

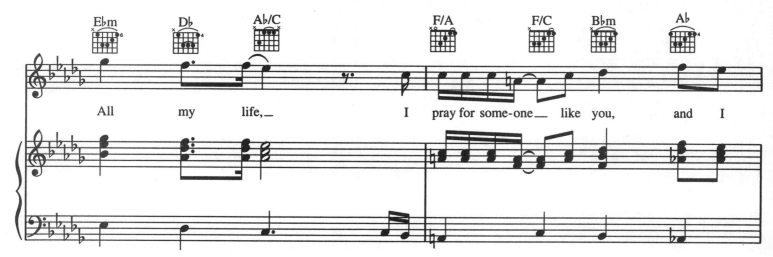

All my life,___ I pray for some-one___ like you, and I

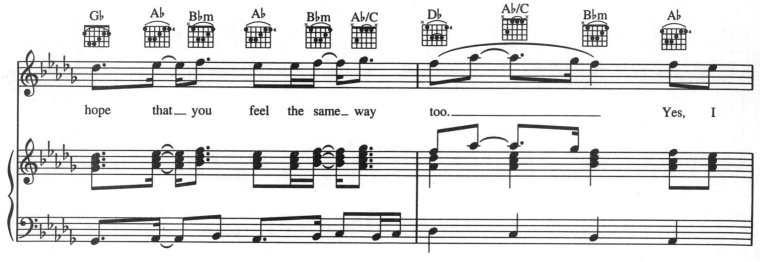

hope that___ you feel the same___ way too._____ Yes, I

pray that___ you do love___ me too.___

2. Say, and I pray that___ you do love___ me. You're

9

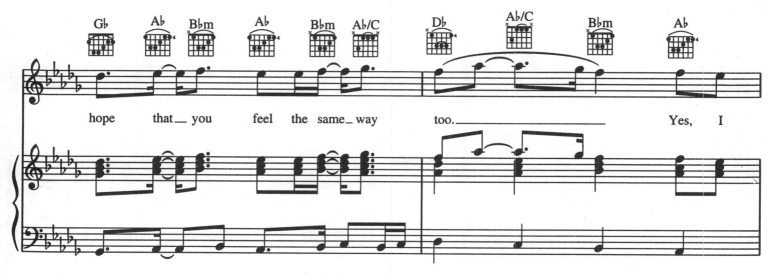

hope that __ you feel the same __ way too. _____ Yes, I

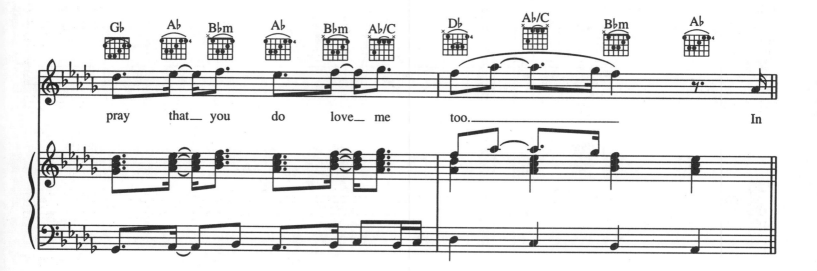

pray that __ you do love __ me too. _____ In

Chorus:

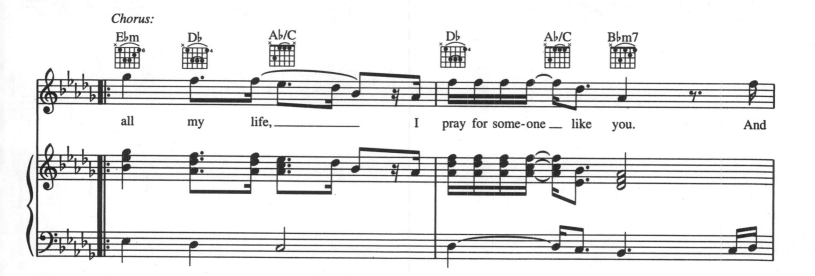

all my life, _____ I pray for some-one __ like you. And

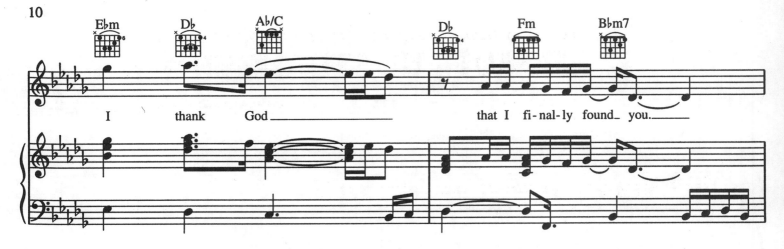

I thank God _____ that I fi-nal-ly found_ you._____

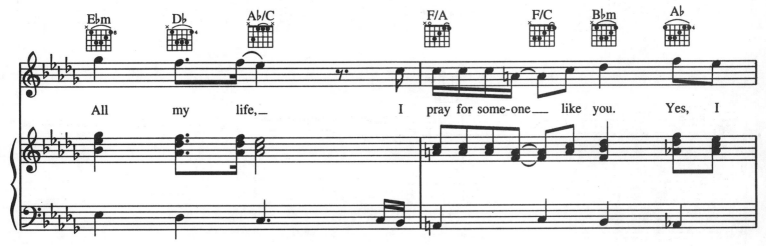

All my life,_ I pray for some-one_ like you. Yes, I

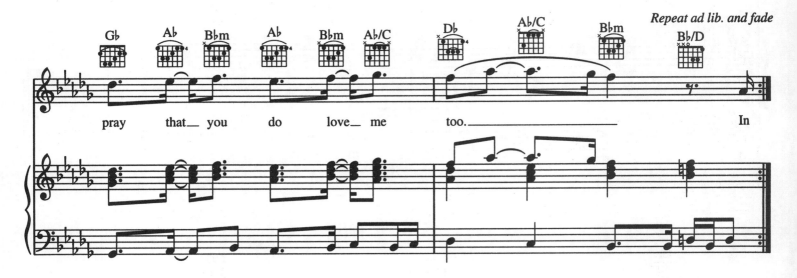

Repeat ad lib. and fade

pray that_ you do love_ me too._____ In

Verse 2:
Say, and I promise to never fall in love with a stranger.
You're all I'm thinkin', love, I praise the Lord above
For sendin' me your love, I cherish every hug.
I really love you so much.
(To Chorus:)

From the Motion Picture AUSTIN POWERS: The Spy Who Shagged Me

BEAUTIFUL STRANGER

Words and Music by
MADONNA CICCONE and WILLIAM ORBIT

14

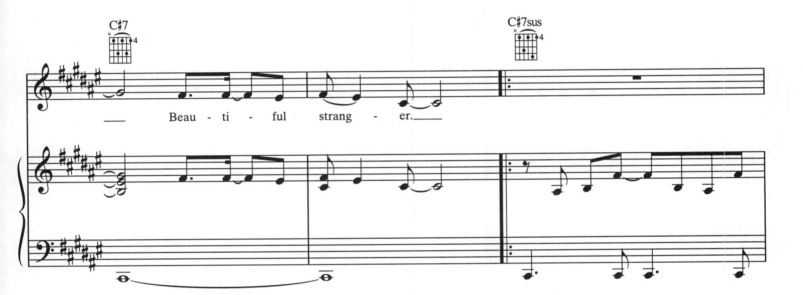

AMAZED

Words and Music by
MARV GREEN, AIMEE MAYO
and CHRIS LINDSEY

Tune guitar down a half step

Slowly ♩ = 76

Verse:

1. Ev - 'ry time our eyes   meet,
2. *See additional lyrics*

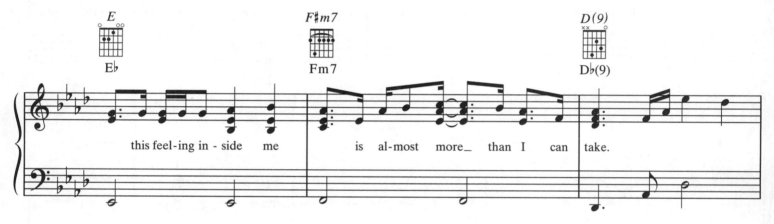

this feel-ing in - side   me   is al-most more__ than I   can   take.

Ba-by, when you touch me,   I can feel how much you love me,   and it just blows__ me a - way.

__   I've nev-er been__ this close to   an-y-one__ or an-y-thing.

I can hear your thoughts, I can see your dreams.

Chorus:

I don't know how you do what you do. I'm so in love with you.

It just keeps get-ting bet - ter.

I wan - na spend the rest of my life with you by my side

for - ev - er and ev - er.

20

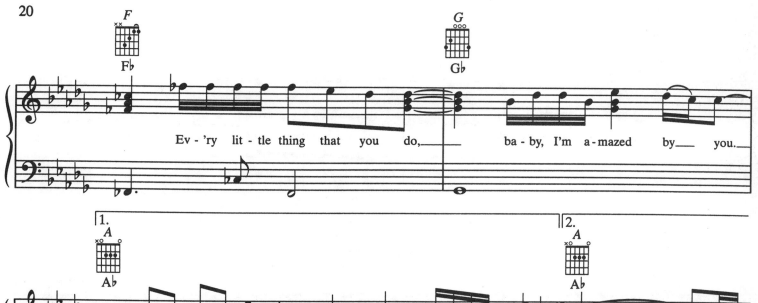

Chorus:

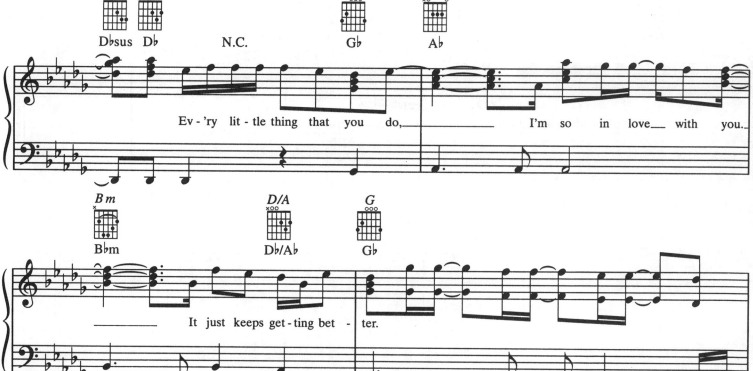

Amazed - 4 - 3

Verse 2:
The smell of your skin,
The taste of your kiss,
The way you whisper in the dark.
Your hair all around me,
Baby, you surround me;
You touch every place in my heart.
Oh, it feels like the first time every time.
I wanna spend the whole night in your eyes.
(To Chorus:)

WHEN I SAID I DO

Words and Music by
CLINT BLACK

Verse 2:
Well, this old world keeps changin'
And the world stays the same
For all who came before.
And it goes hand in hand,
Only you and I can undo
All that we became.
That makes us so much more

Than a woman and a man.
And after everything that comes and goes around
Has only passed us by,
Here alone in our dreams,
I know there's a lonely heart in every lost and found.
But forever you and I will be the ones
Who found out what forever means.
(To Chorus:)

AS TIME GOES BY

Words and Music by
HERMAN HUPFELD

As Time Goes By - 4 - 1

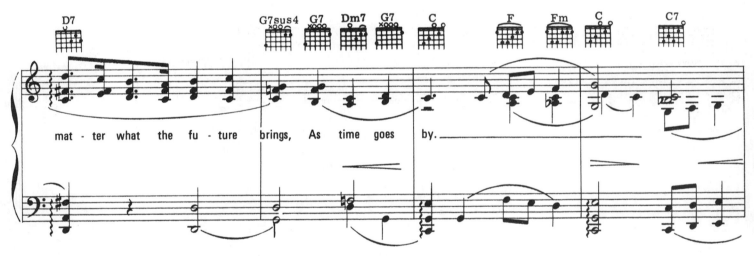

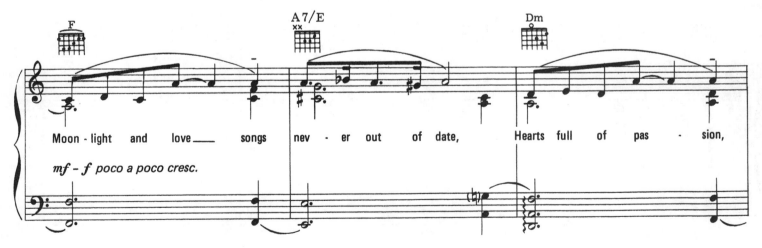

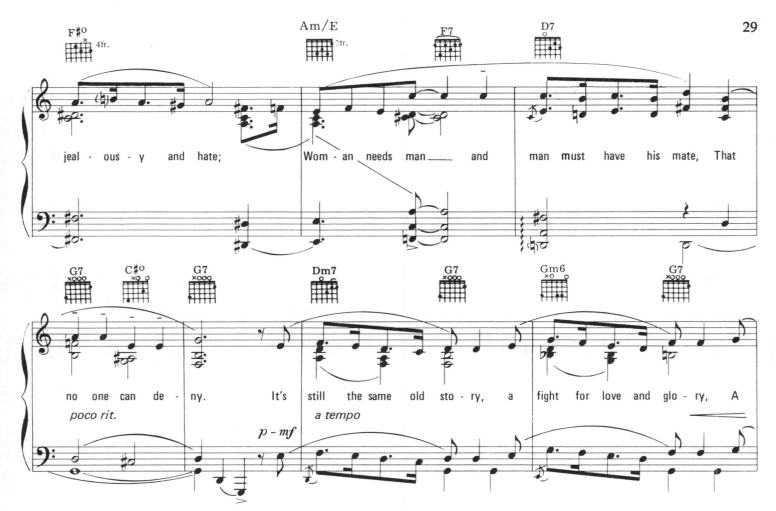

jeal - ous - y and hate; Wom - an needs man___ and man must have his mate, That

no one can de - ny. It's still the same old sto - ry, a fight for love and glo - ry, A

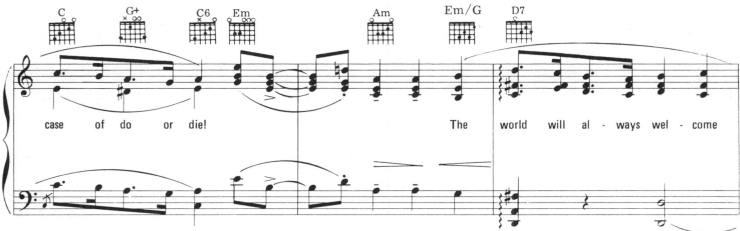

case of do or die! The world will al - ways wel - come

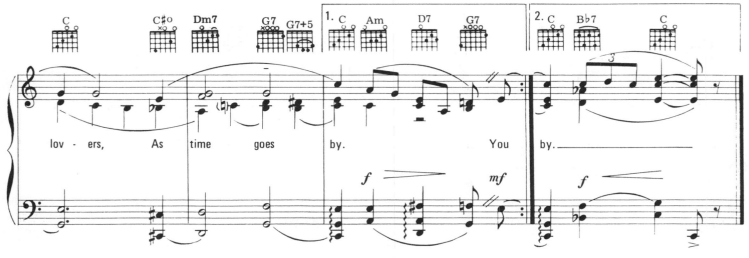

lov - ers, As time goes by. You by.____

...BABY ONE MORE TIME

Words and Music by
MAX MARTIN

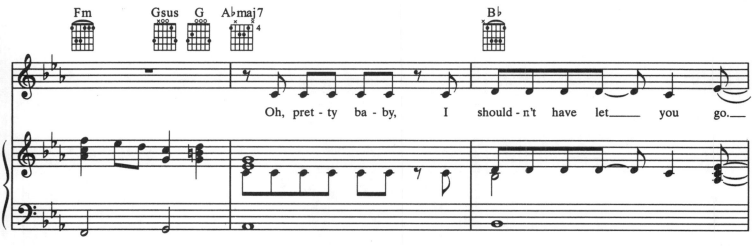

Oh, pret - ty ba - by, I should - n't have let___ you go.___

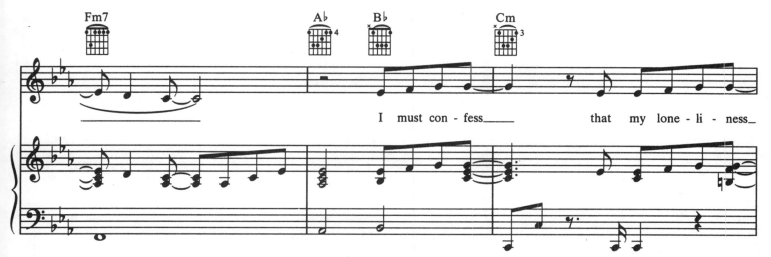

I must con - fess___ that my lone - li - ness___

___ is kill - ing me now._____ Don't you know I still___ be - lieve_

___ that you will be here___ and give me a sign.___ Hit me, ba - by, one more time.

. . . Baby One More Time - 5 - 4

34

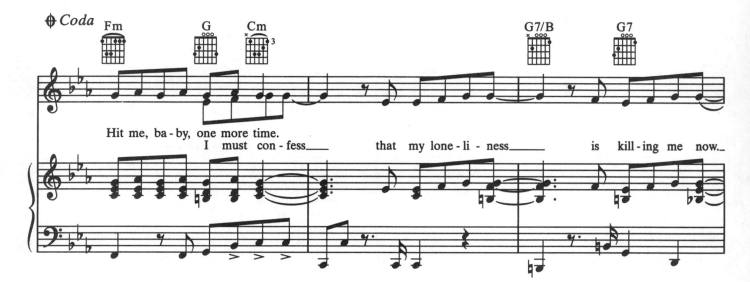

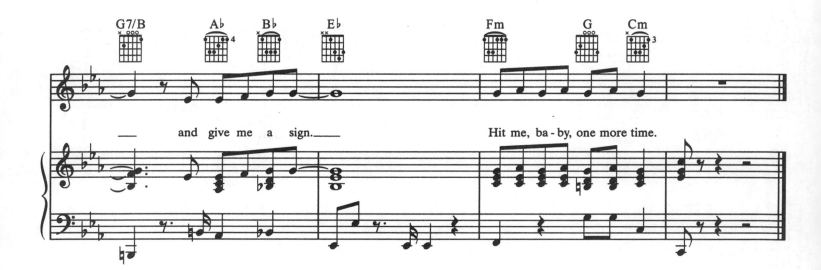

WHAT A FOOL BELIEVES

Words and Music by
KENNY LOGGINS and MICHAEL McDONALD

He came from some-where back in her long__ a-go,__ the sen-ti-men-tal fool don't see, try-in' hard __ to re-cre-ate what had yet __

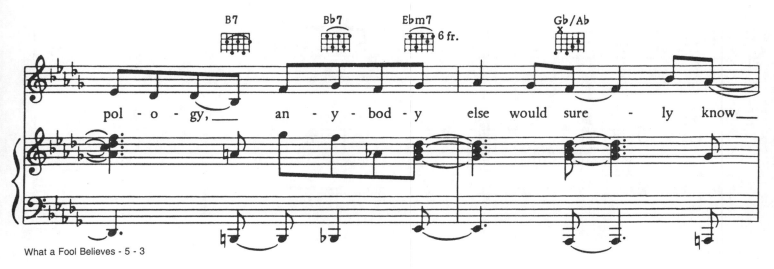

What a Fool Believes - 5 - 3

What seems _____ to be____ is

al - ways bet -ter than noth - ing. And noth-ing at all___

keeps send-ing him   What a fool___ be-lieves.

D. S. 𝄋 and fade

he___ sees,___   no wise man has the pow-

What a Fool Believes - 5 - 5

BECAUSE YOU LOVED ME
(Theme from "Up Close & Personal")

Words and Music by
DIANE WARREN

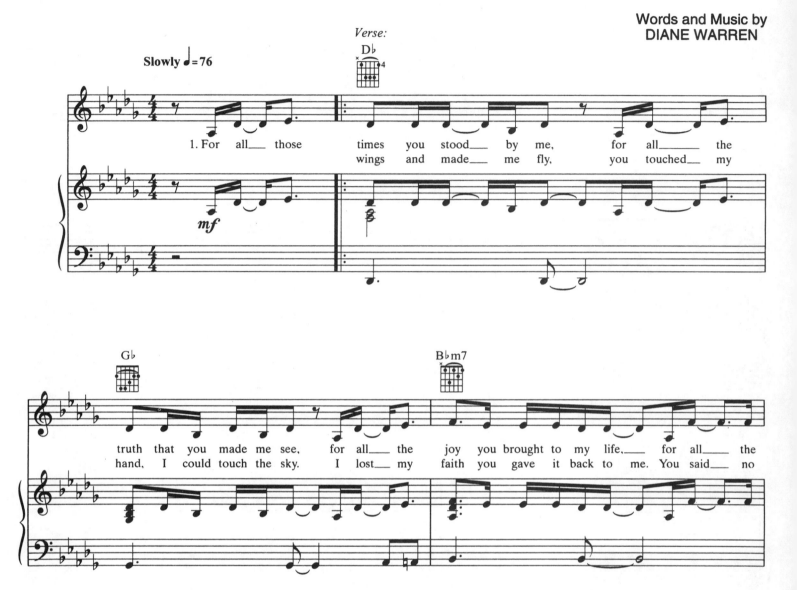

Slowly ♩ = 76   *Verse:*

1. For all___ those times you stood___ by me, for all___ the
wings and made___ me fly, you touched___ my

truth that you made me see, for all___ the joy you brought to my life,___ for all___ the
hand, I could touch the sky. I lost___ my faith you gave it back to me. You said___ no

wrong that you___ made right, for ev - ery___ dream you made___ come true, for all___ the
star was out___ of reach, you stood___ by___ me and I___ stood tall. I had___ your

Because You Loved Me - 5 - 1

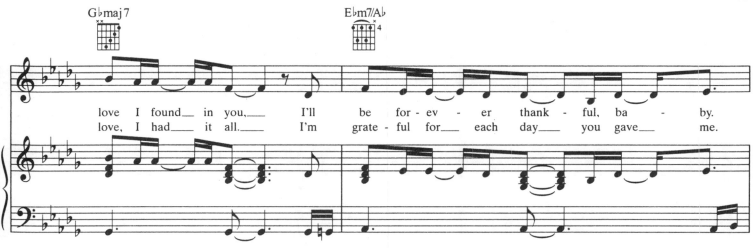

love I found__ in you,__ I'll be for - ev - er thank - ful, ba - by.
love, I had__ it all.__ I'm grate - ful for__ each day__ you gave__ me.

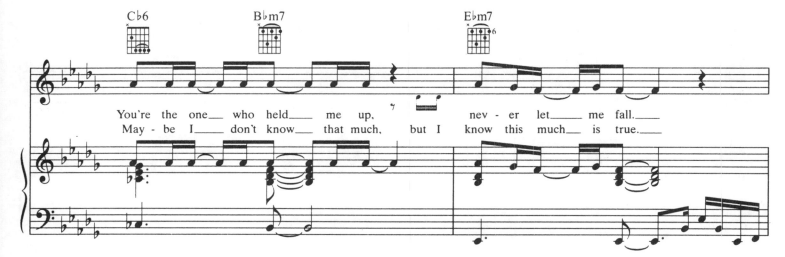

You're the one__ who held__ me up, nev - er let__ me fall.__
May - be I__ don't know__ that much, but I know this much__ is true.__

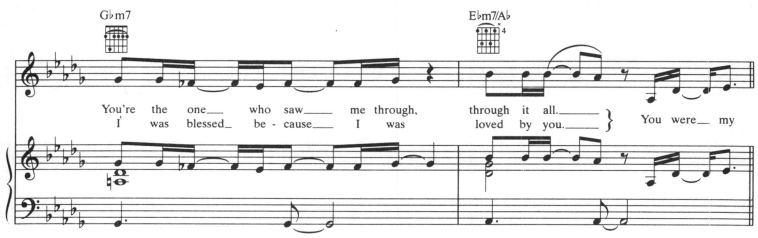

You're the one__ who saw__ me through, through it all.__ You were__ my
I was blessed_ be - cause__ I was loved by you.__

Chorus:

strength when I__ was weak, you were__ my voice when I could - n't speak. You were__ my

Because You Loved Me - 5 - 2

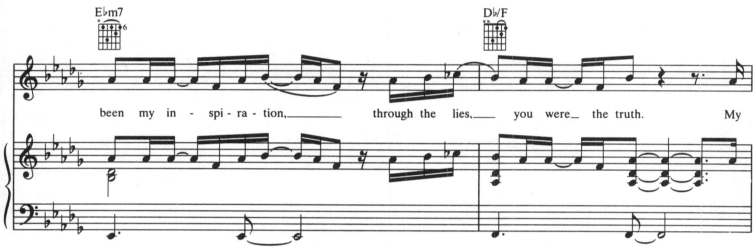

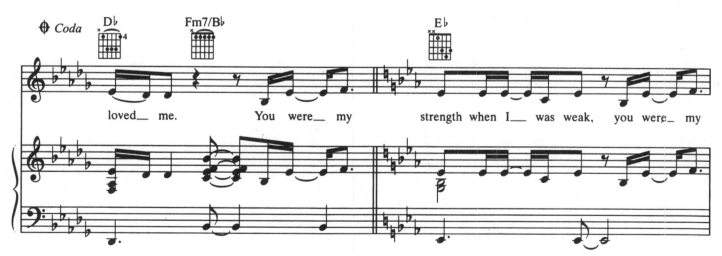

Because You Loved Me - 5 - 4

44

voice when I could-n't speak. You were__ my eyes when I could-n't see, you saw__ the

best there was__ in me, lift-ed__ me__ up when I could-n't reach. You gave__ me

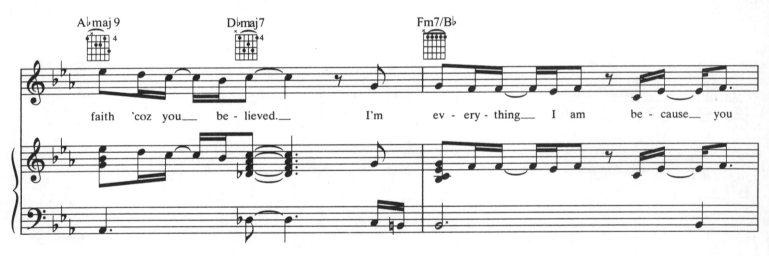

faith 'coz you__ be-lieved.__ I'm ev-ery-thing__ I am be-cause__ you

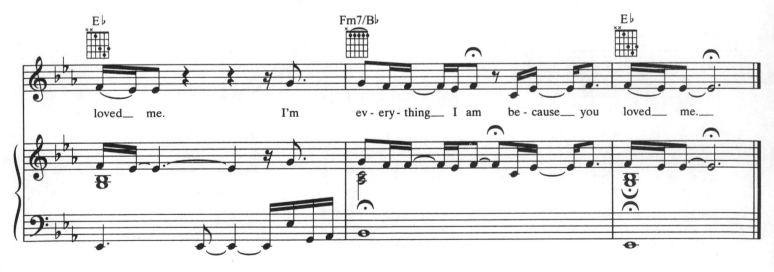

loved__ me. I'm ev-ery-thing__ I am be-cause__ you loved__ me.__

MOONDANCE

Words and Music by
VAN MORRISON

46

tab - u - lous night___ to make ro - mance 'neath the cov - er of Oc - to - ber
know now the time___ is just___ right and straight in - to my arms___ you will

skies.
run. And all the leaves on the trees are fall - ing to the
And when you come, my heart will be wait - ing to make

sound of the breez - es that blow. And I'm try - ing to please___ to the call -
sure that you're nev - er a - lone. There and then all my dreams___ will come true,___

ing of your heart - strings that play soft and low. And all the
___ dear, there and then will I make you my own. And ev - 'ry

Moondance - 5 - 2

48

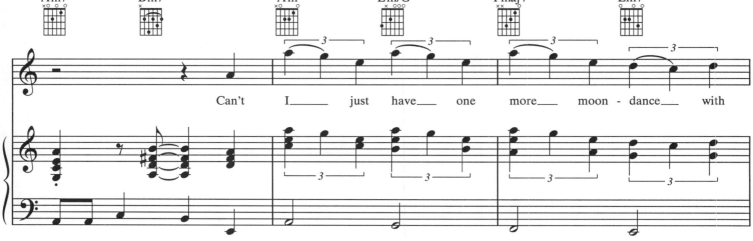

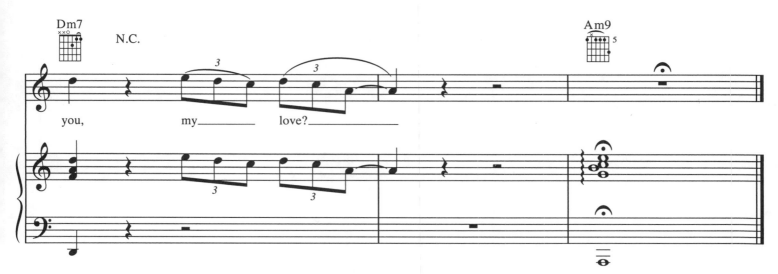

DANCING QUEEN

Words and Music by
BENNY ANDERSSON, STIG ANDERSON
and BJÖRN ULVAEUS

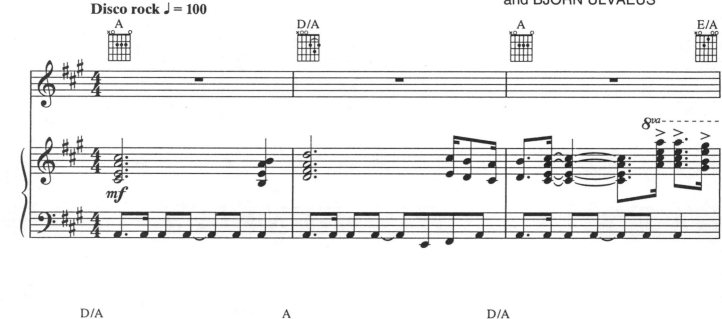

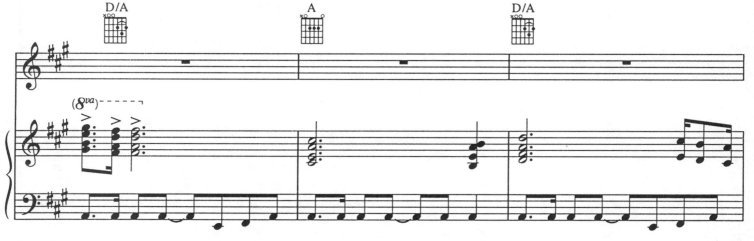

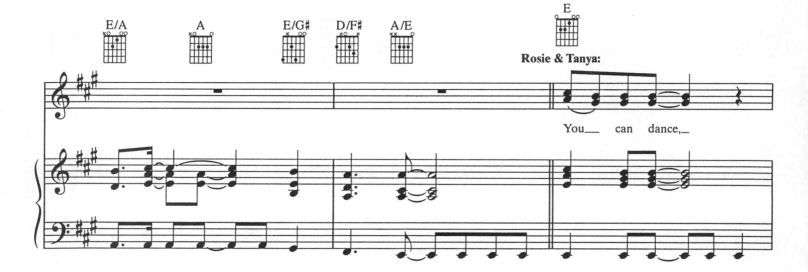

Rosie & Tanya:

You__ can dance,__

Dancing Queen - 7 - 1

Dancing Queen - 7 - 2

Chorus:

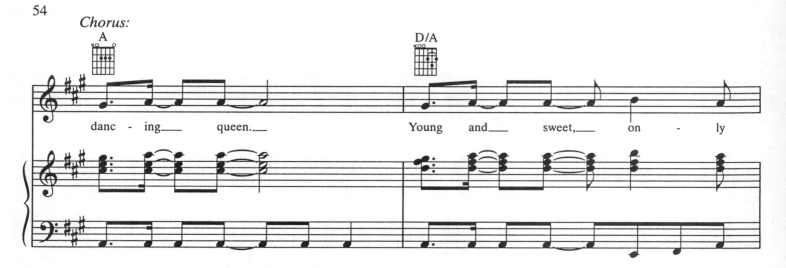

danc - ing____ queen.____ Young and____ sweet,____ on - ly

sev - en - teen._____ Danc - ing____ queen,____

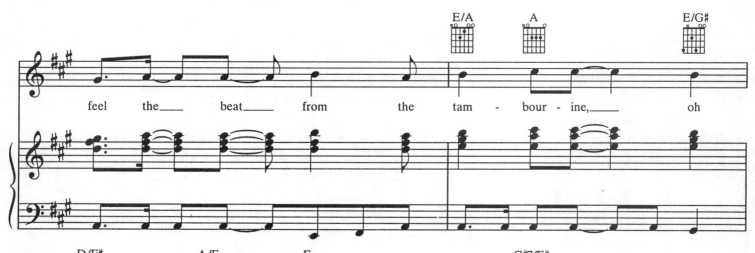

feel the____ beat____ from the tam - bour - ine,____ oh

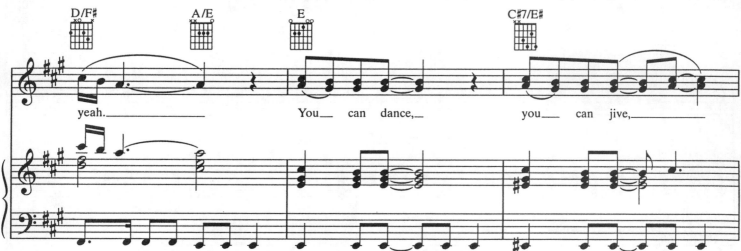

yeah._____ You__ can dance,__ you__ can jive,____

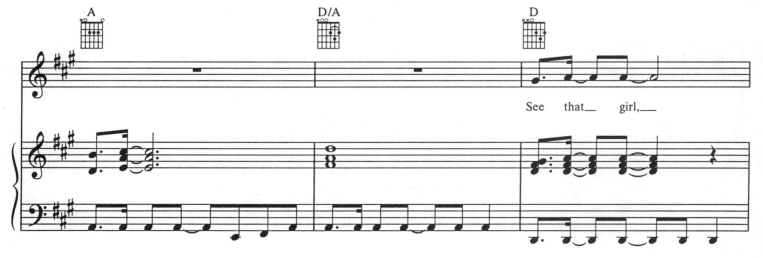

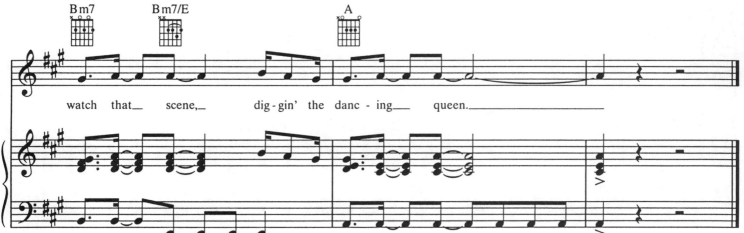

THE DANCE

Words and Music by
TONY ARATA

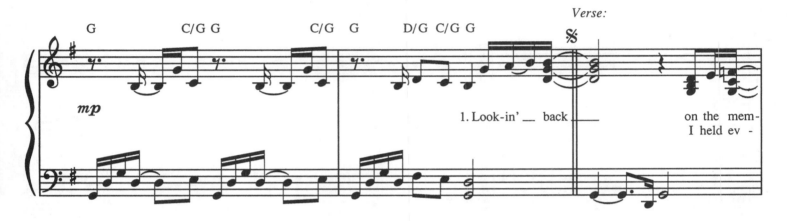

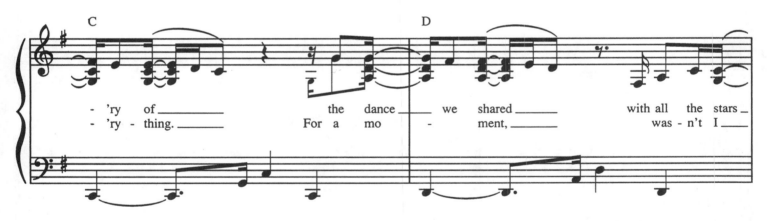

The Dance - 3 - 1

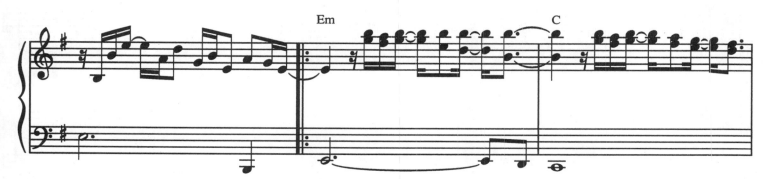

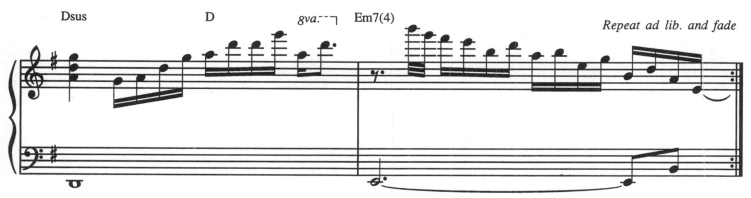

The Dance - 3 - 3

BYE BYE BYE

Words and Music by KRISTIAN LUNDIN,
JAKE and ANDREAS CARLSSON

Bye Bye Bye - 4 - 1

CAT'S IN THE CRADLE

Moderately, with a 2 feel ♩ = 76

Words and Music by
HARRY CHAPIN and SANDY CHAPIN

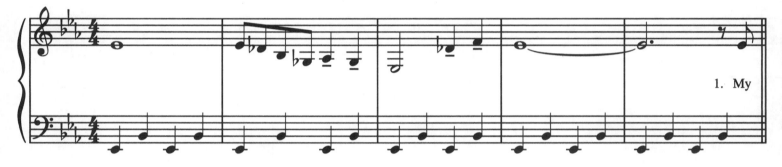

1. My

Verses 1 & 2:

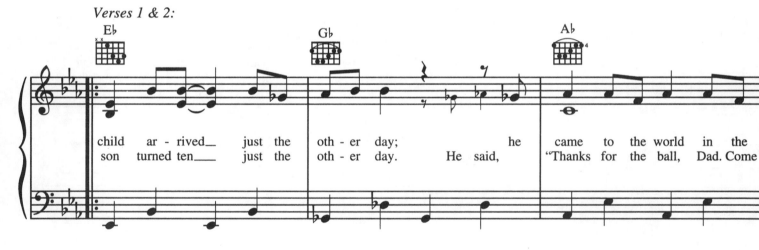

child ar-rived___ just the oth-er day; he came to the world in the
son turned ten___ just the oth-er day. He said, "Thanks for the ball, Dad. Come

u-su-al way.___ But there were planes to catch___ and bills to pay.___
on, let's play.___ Can you teach me to throw?"___ I said, "Not to-day.___ I got a

Cat's in the Cradle - 6 - 1

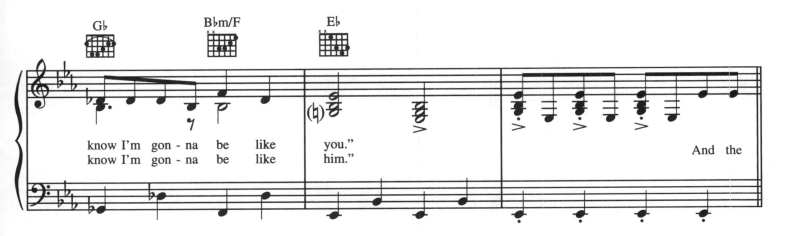

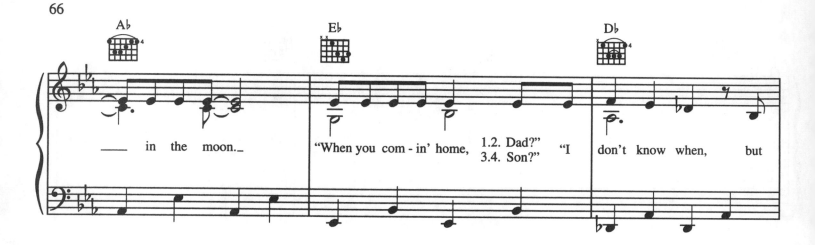

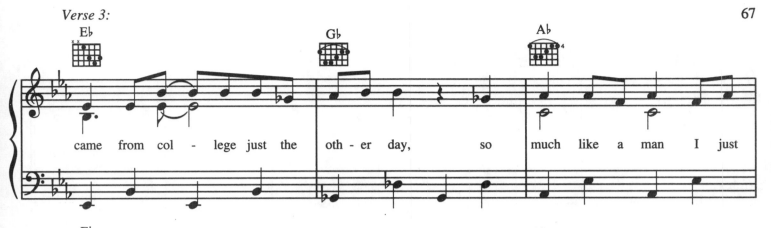

came from col - lege just the oth - er day, so much like a man I just

had to say,___ "Son, I'm proud of you.___ Can you sit for a while?"_ He

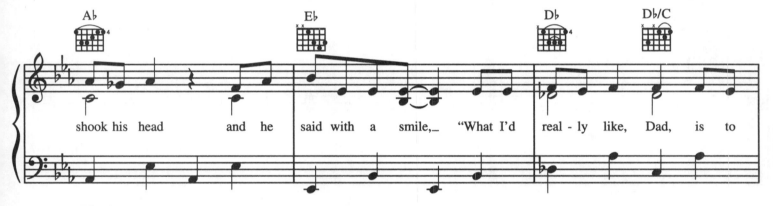

shook his head and he said with a smile,_ "What I'd real - ly like, Dad, is to

D.S. 𝄋 *al Coda I*

bor-row the car___ keys. See you lat - er. Can I have them, please?" And the

⊕ *Coda I*

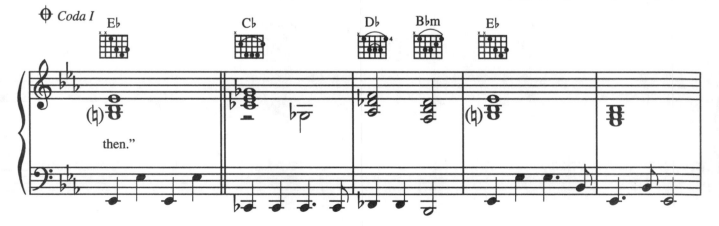

then."

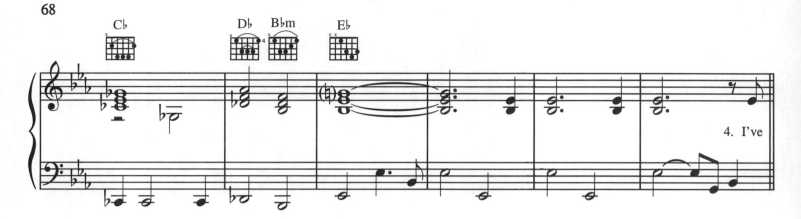

Verse 4:

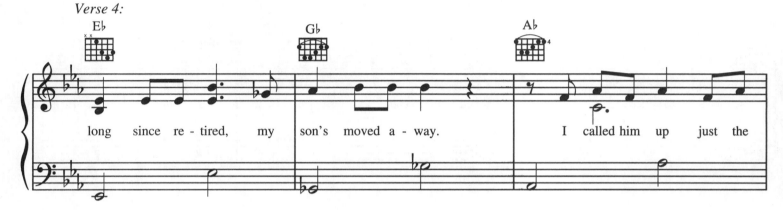

4. I've

long since re-tired, my son's moved a-way. I called him up just the

oth-er day. I said, "I'd like to see__ you if you don't mind."_ He said, "I'd

love to, Dad,__ if I can find the time.__ You see, my

new job's a has-sle and the kids have the flu,__ but it's sure nice talk-in' to

THIS KISS

Words and Music by
ROBIN LERNER, ANNIE ROBOFF
and BETH NIELSEN CHAPMAN

Moderately, with double-time feel ♩ = 64

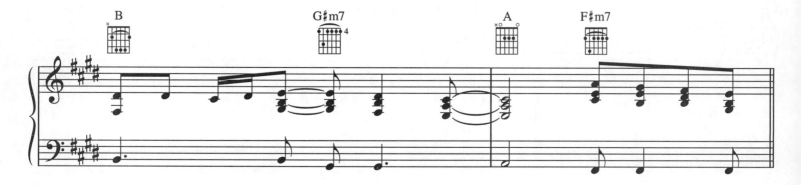

Verse:

1. I don't want an-oth-er heart-break. I don't need an-oth-er turn to cry,_____ no.
2. Cin-der-el-la said to Snow White, "How does love get so off course?"_____ Oh.

I don't want to learn the hard way. Ba-by, hel-lo, oh no, good-bye.
All I want-ed was a white knight with a good heart, soft touch, fast horse.

This Kiss - 4 - 1

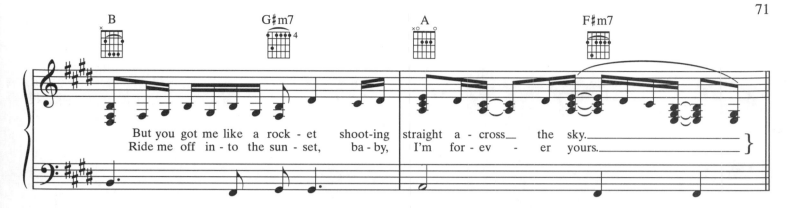

But you got me like a rock - et shoot-ing straight a - cross __ the sky. ___
Ride me off in - to the sun - set, ba - by, I'm for - ev - er yours. ___

Chorus:

It's the way __ you love me. It's a feel-ing like this. __

It's cen - trif - u - gal mo - tion. It's per - pet - u - al bliss. __

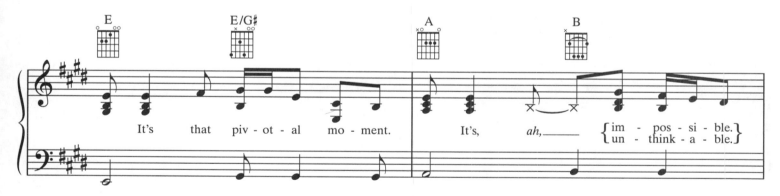

It's that piv - ot - al mo - ment. It's, *ah,* __ {im - pos - si - ble. / un - think - a - ble.}

This kiss, __ this kiss, __ {un - stop - a - ble. / un - sink - a - ble.}

72

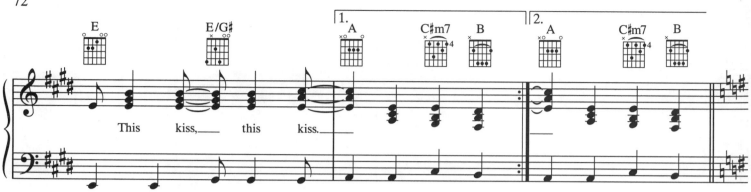

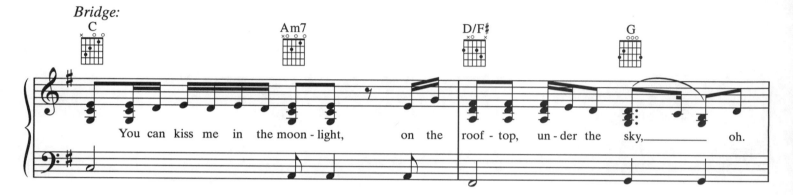

Bridge:

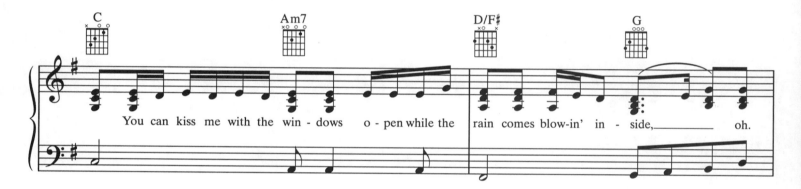

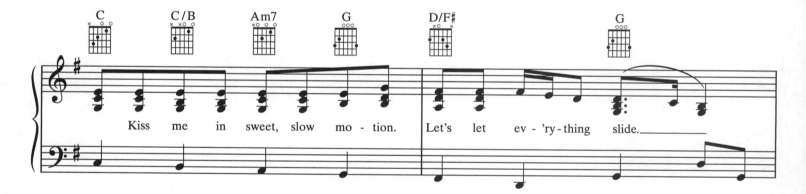

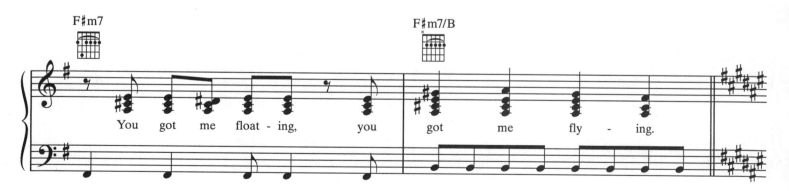

This Kiss - 4 - 3

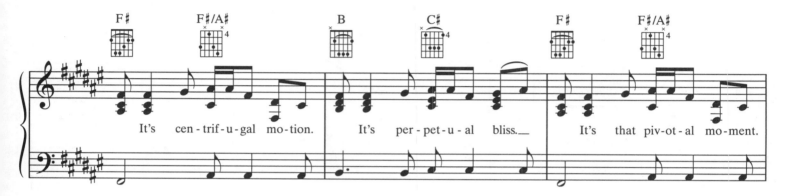

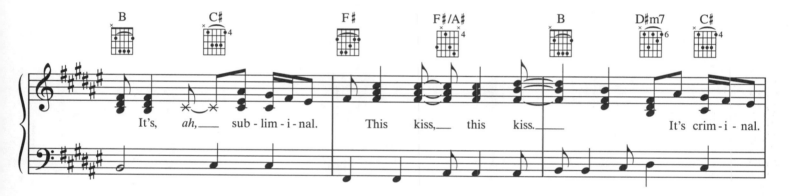

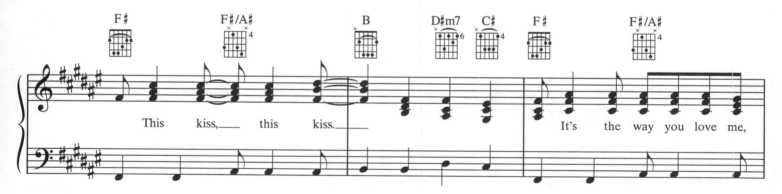

Repeat and fade

DESPERADO

Words and Music by
DON HENLEY and GLENN FREY

Desperado - 6 - 1

so long now.__ Oh, you're a hard one, I know that

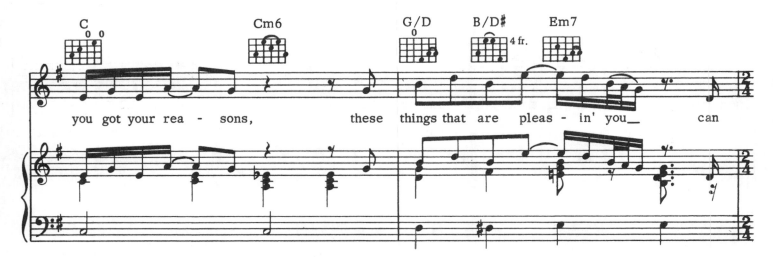

you got your rea - sons, these things that are pleas - in' you__ can

hurt you some-how. Don't you draw the queen__ of dia - monds,__ boy,__ she'll

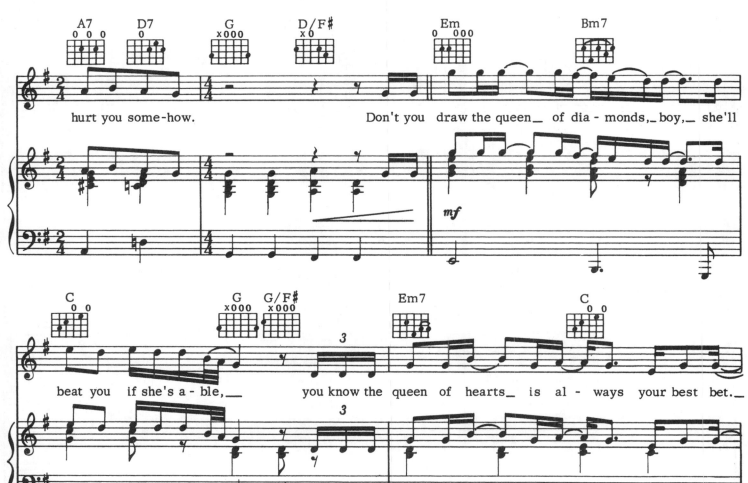

beat you if she's a - ble,__ you know the queen of hearts__ is al - ways your best bet.__

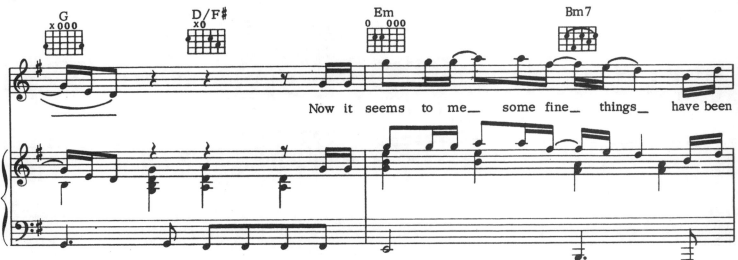

Now it seems to me_ some fine_ things_ have been

laid up-on_ your ta - ble, but you on - ly want_ the ones_ that you can't_ get._

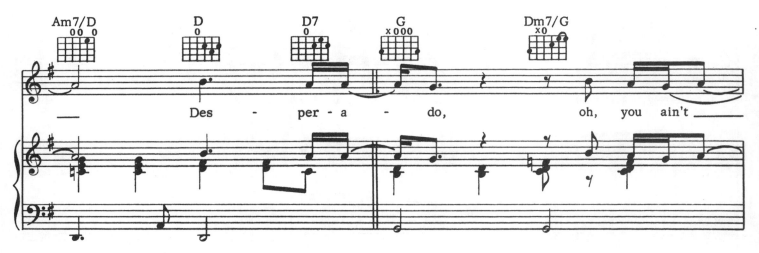

_ Des - per - a - do, oh, you ain't _____

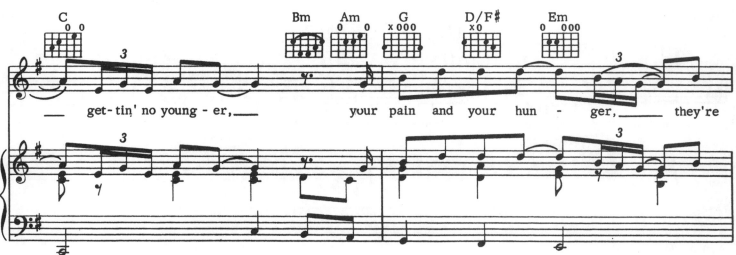

_ get-tin' no young - er,___ your pain and your hun - ger,____ they're

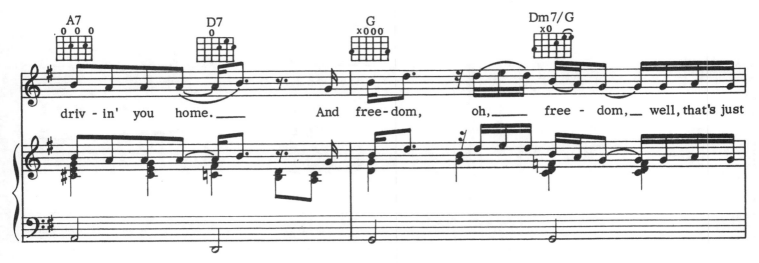

driv - in' you home.___ And free - dom, oh,____ free - dom,__ well, that's just

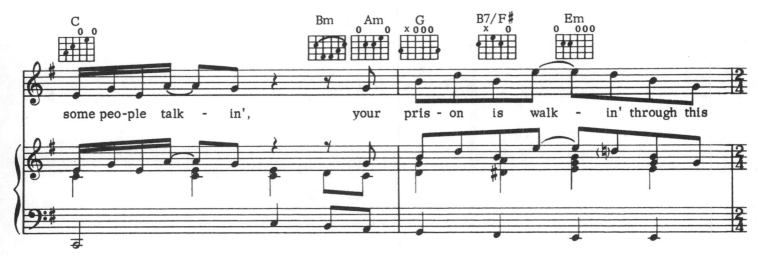

some peo - ple talk - in', your pris - on is walk - in' through this

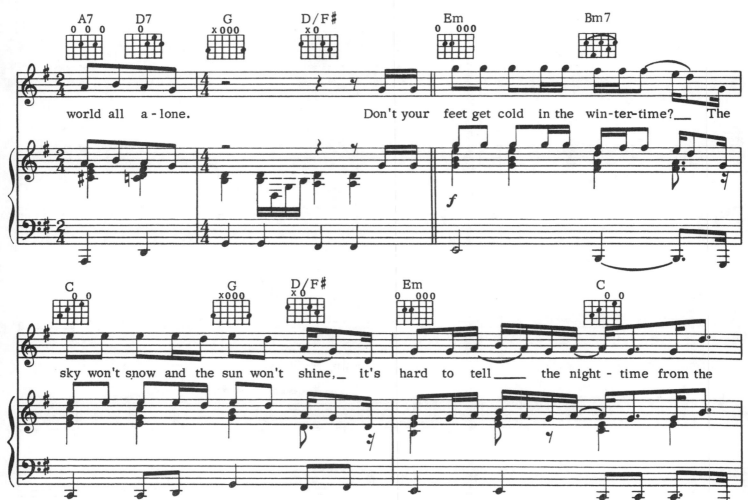

world all a - lone. Don't your feet get cold in the win - ter - time?___ The

sky won't snow and the sun won't shine,_ it's hard to tell____ the night - time from the

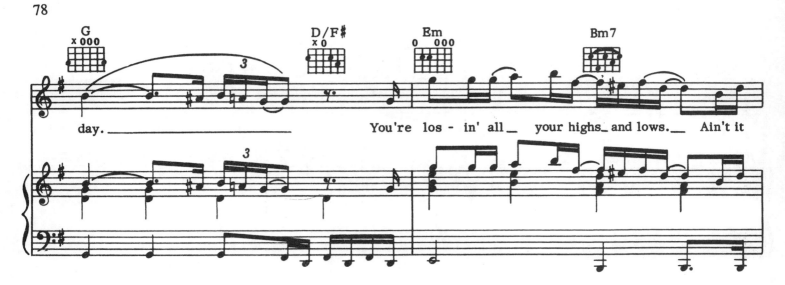

day. _____ You're los - in' all _ your highs _ and lows. _ Ain't it

fun-ny how _ the feel - in' goes _ a - way? _____

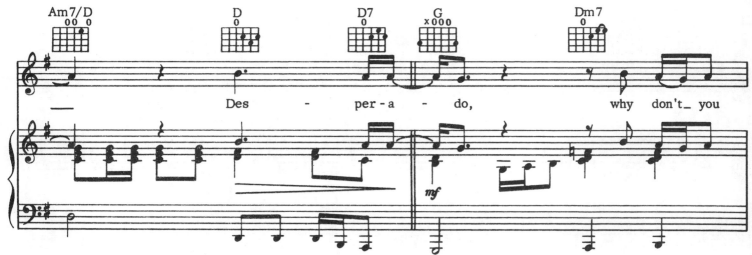

_ Des - per - a - do, why don't _ you

come to your sens - es? Come down from your fenc - es, ____

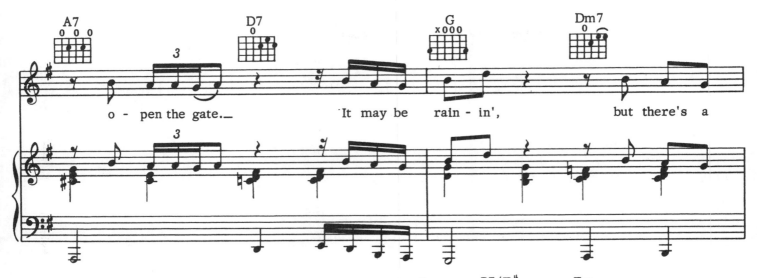

o - pen the gate.___ It may be rain - in', but there's a

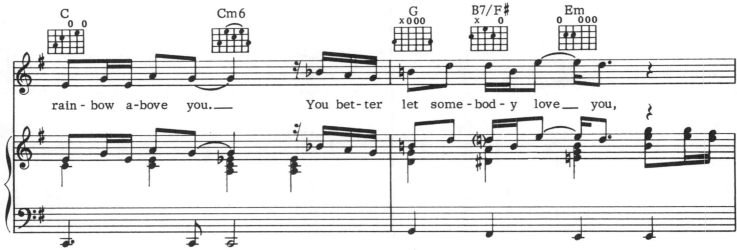

rain - bow a-bove you.___ You bet-ter let some-bod-y love___ you,

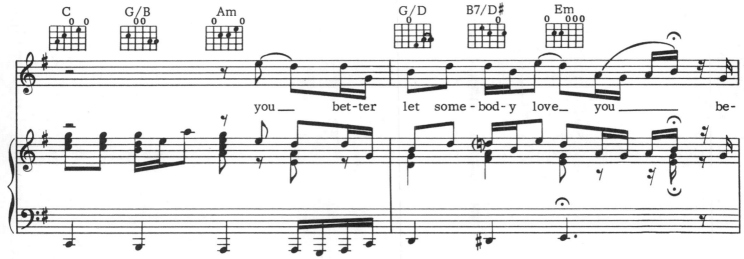

you___ bet-ter let some-bod-y love___ you _____ be-

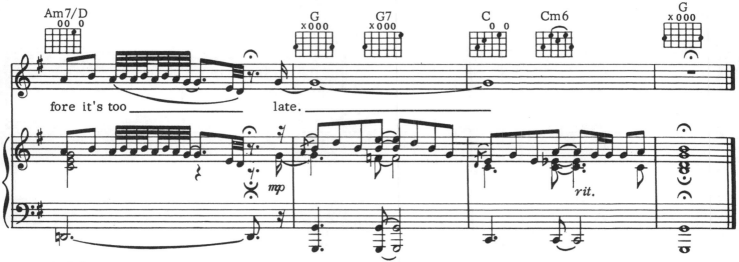

fore it's too _____ late.

Desperado - 6 - 6

HEAVEN KNOWS

Words and Music by
DONNA SUMMER, GIORGIO MORODER,
PETE BELLOTTE and GREG MATHIESON

Moderately - hard beat

Heaven Knows - 4 - 1

Coda

Heav - en knows ___ it's not the way it should be, I just

had to stop, ___ I had to stop pre-tend-ing, so come on now, ___

hear me when I cry. _____

EVERGREEN
Love Theme from "A Star Is Born"

Words by
PAUL WILLIAMS

Music by
BARBRA STREISAND

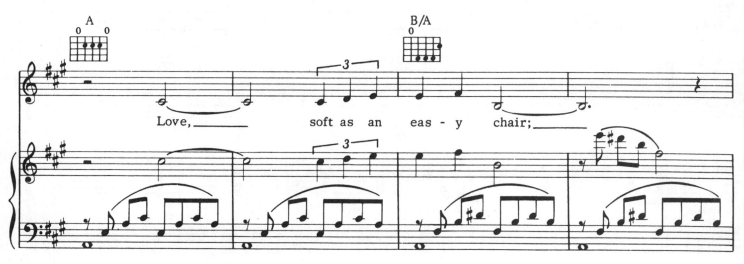

Evergreen - 6 - 1

love, _____ fresh as the morn-ing air. _____

One _____ love that is shared by two, _____

I have found _____ with you. _____

___ Like a rose _____ un-der the A-pril snow, ___

Evergreen - 6 - 2

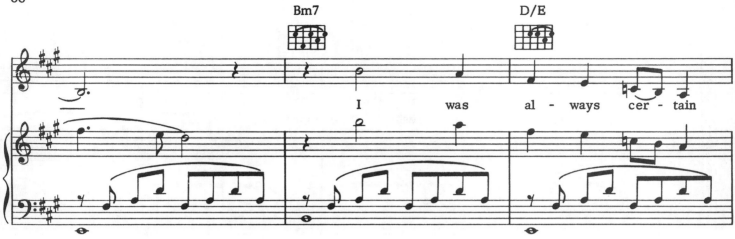

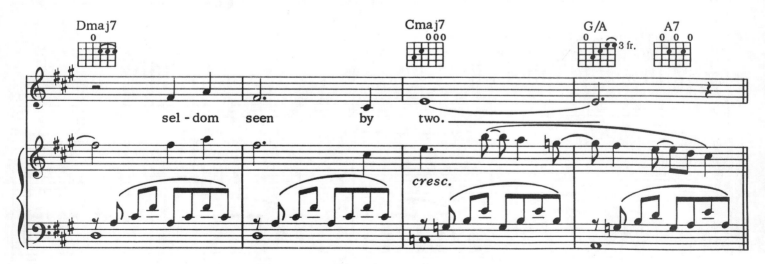

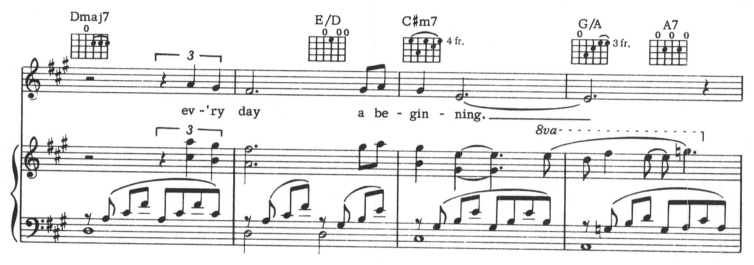

Evergreen - 6 - 4

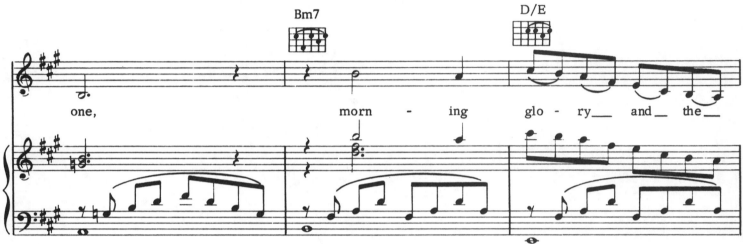

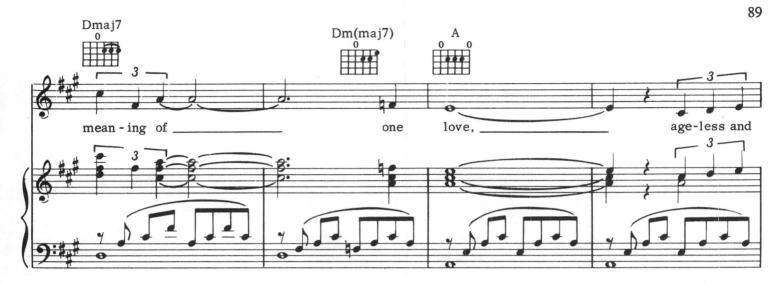

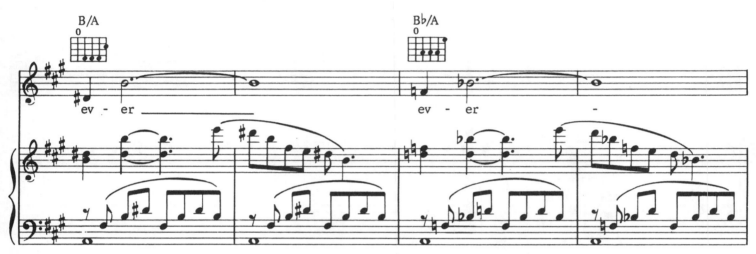

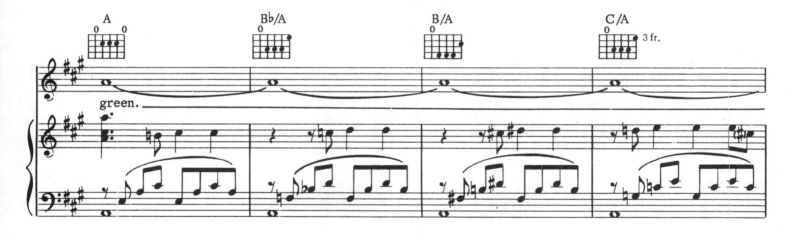

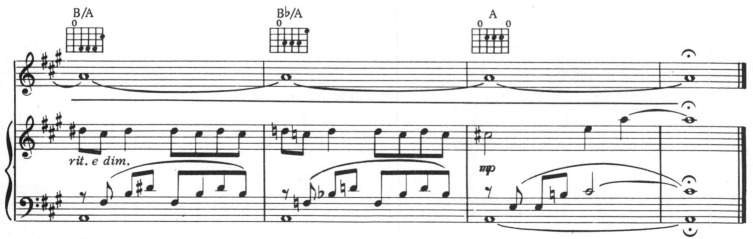

SOMEONE SAVED MY LIFE TONIGHT

Words and Music by
ELTON JOHN and BERNIE TAUPIN

Slowly

Verse

1. When I think of those east end lights, mug-gy nights, the cur-tains drawn in the lit - tle room down stairs Pri-ma-don-na, lord you real-ly should have been there. sit-ting like a prin-cess perched in her e-lec-tric chair. And it's

Someone Saved My Life Tonight - 5 - 1

save your strength— and run the field you play a-lone.—

Some-one saved, some-one saved, some-one saved my life— to-night.—

ADDITIONAL LYRICS

Verse 2.

I never realised the passing hours
Of evening showers,
A slip noose hanging in my darkest dreams.
I'm strangled by your haunted social scene
Just a pawn out-played by a dominating queen.
It's four-o-clock in the morning
Damn it!
Listen to me good.
I'm sleeping with myself tonight
Saved in time, thank God my music's still alive.

To Chorus.

FOOLISH GAMES

Words and Music by
JEWEL KILCHER

Moderately slow ♩ = 66

with pedal

1. You took____ your___ coat off____ and stood in the

2.3.4. *See additional lyrics*

rain,____ you're al-ways cra - zy like_ that.

And I watched_ from my___ win - dow, al-ways felt I was

* *Vocal sung one octave lower*

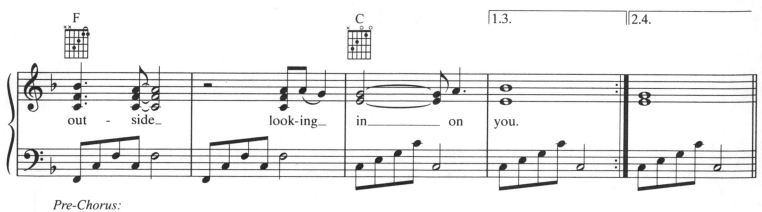

out - side_ look-ing_ in_____ on you.

Pre-Chorus:

1. In case_ you failed to no-tice, in case you failed to see,
2. *See additional lyrics*

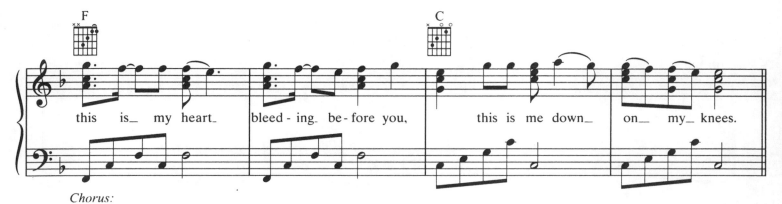

this is_ my heart_ bleed-ing_ be-fore you, this is me down_ on_ my_ knees.

Chorus:

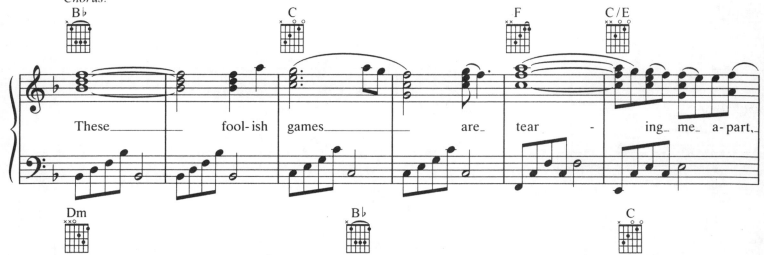

These_____ fool-ish games_____ are_ tear - ing_ me_ a-part,

_____ and your___ thought-less words_____

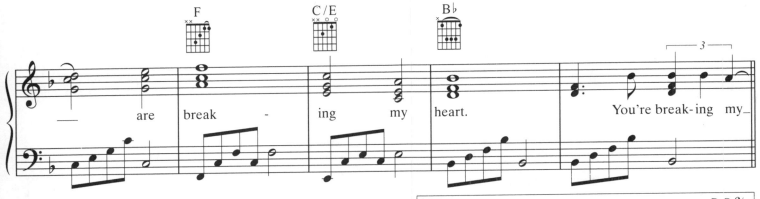

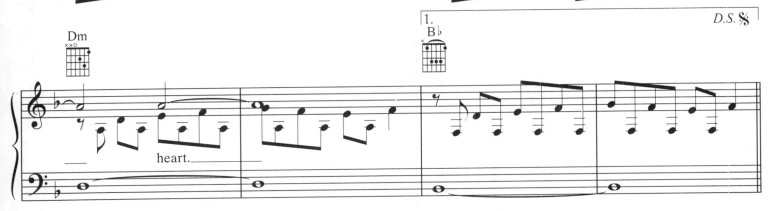

Verse 2:
You're always the mysterious one with
Dark eyes and careless hair,
You were fashionably sensitive
But too cool to care.
You stood in my doorway with nothing to say
Besides some comment on the weather.
(To Pre-Chorus:)

Verse 3:
You're always brilliant in the morning,
Smoking your cigarettes and talking over coffee.
Your philosophies on art, Baroque moved you.
You loved Mozart and you'd speak of your loved ones
As I clumsily strummed my guitar.

Verse 4:
You'd teach me of honest things,
Things that were daring, things that were clean.
Things that knew what an honest dollar did mean.
I hid my soiled hands behind my back.
Somewhere along the line, I must have gone
Off track with you.

Pre-Chorus 2:
Excuse me, think I've mistaken you for somebody else,
Somebody who gave a damn, somebody more like myself.
(To Chorus:)

WORDS

Words and Music by
BARRY GIBB, MAURICE GIBB
and ROBIN GIBB

Smile an ev-er-last-ing smile; a smile could bring you near to me. Don't ev-er let me find you

Words - 4 - 1

gone 'cause that would bring a tear to me.   This

world has lost its glo - ry;   let's start a brand - new sto - ry

now,   my love.   Right now,   there'll be no oth - er

time,   and I can show you how,   my   love. ___

100

Talk in ev - er - last - ing words and ded - i - cate them all to me.

And I will give you all my life, I'm here if you should

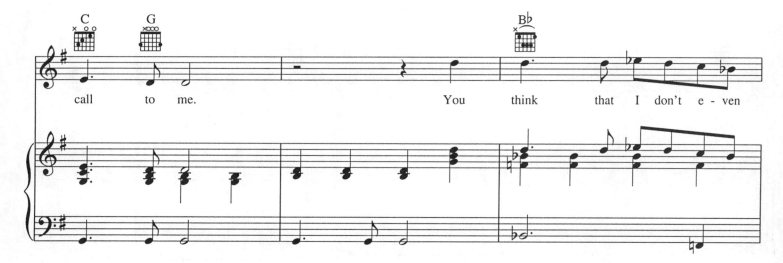

call to me. You think that I don't e - ven

mean a sin - gle word I say. It's on - ly

Words - 4 - 3

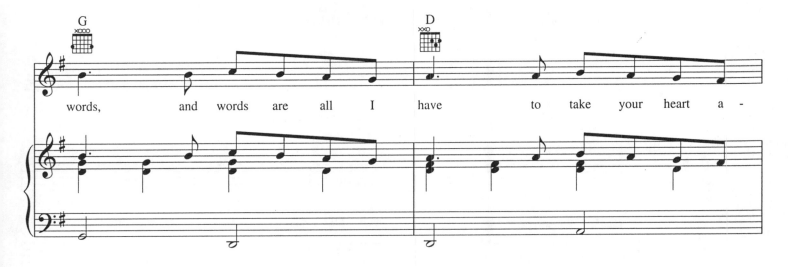

words, and words are all I have to take your heart a-

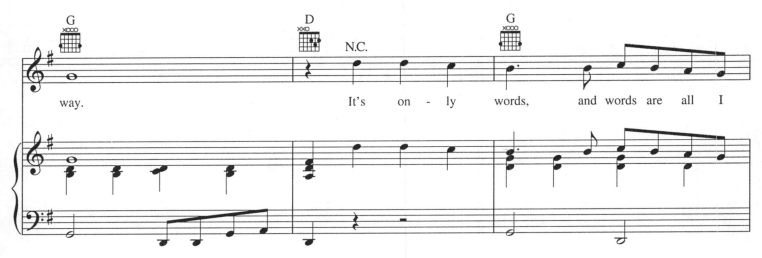

way. It's on-ly words, and words are all I

have to take your heart a-way. It's on-ly

words, and words are all I have to take your heart a-way.

rit.

FROM THIS MOMENT ON

Words and Music by
SHANIA TWAIN and R.J. LANGE

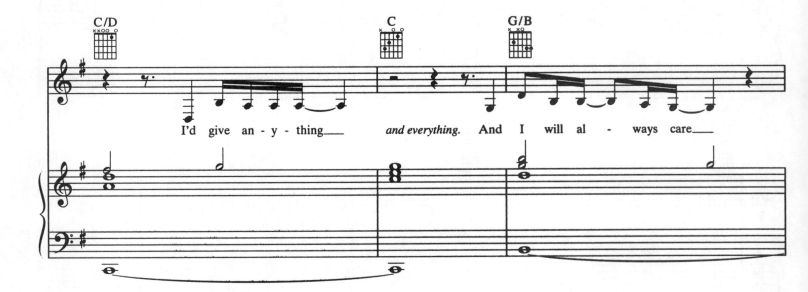

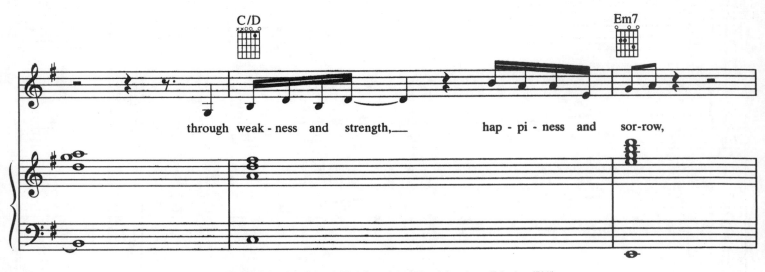

From This Moment On - 7 - 1

wait to live_ my life_ with you,_ can't wait to start._ You and I__ will nev - er be__ a-

part._____ My dreams_ came true_____ be - cause_

__ of you._____ 3. From this mo - ment, as long as I live,_

__ I will love you,_____ I prom - ise you this._____ There is noth-

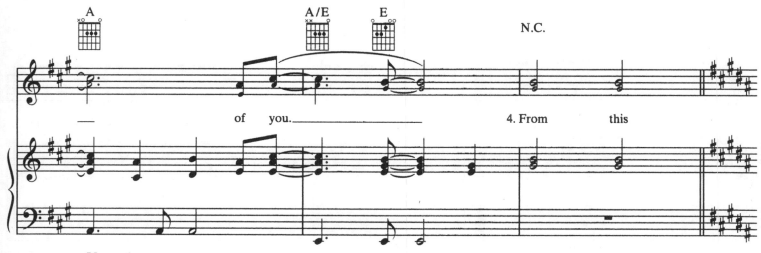

Verse 4:

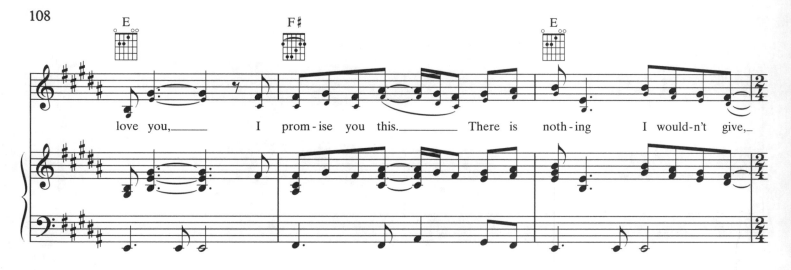

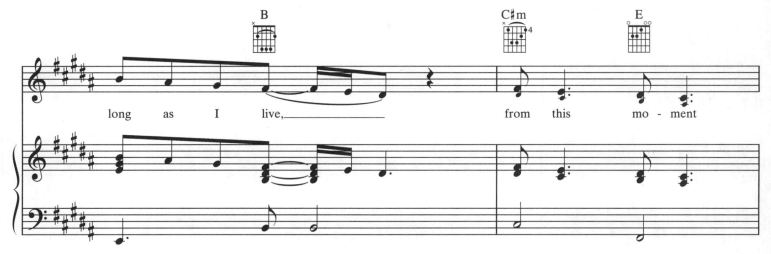

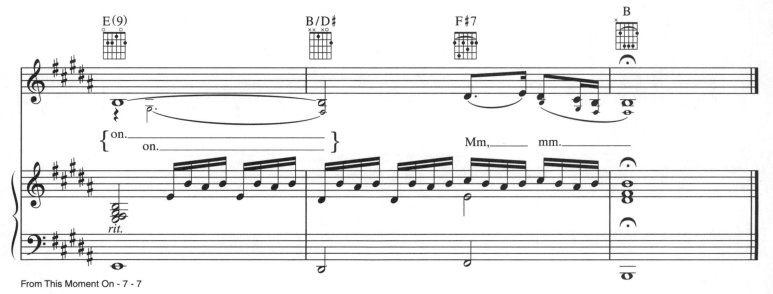

GOOD RIDDANCE
(Time of Your Life)

Words and Music by
BILLIE JOE ARMSTRONG, FRANK WRIGHT
and MICHAEL PRITCHARD

1. An-oth-er turn-ing point,__ a fork__ stuck in__ the__ road.
2. So take the pho-to-graphs and still-frames__ in your__ mind.
3. (Inst. solo ad lib....

Time grabs you by__ the__ wrist, di-rects__ you where__ to__ go.
Hang it on__ a__ shelf__ in good__ health and__ good__ time.

Good Riddance - 3 - 1

Good Riddance - 3 - 2

THE GREATEST LOVE OF ALL

Words by
LINDA CREED

Music by
MICHAEL MASSER

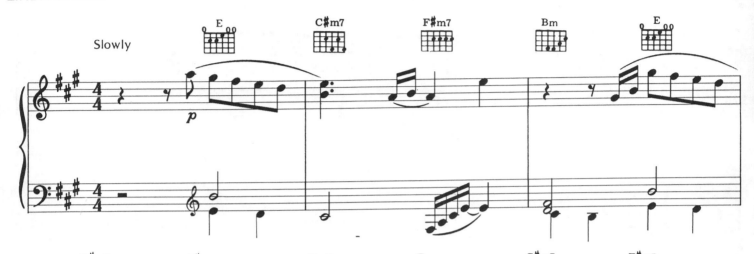

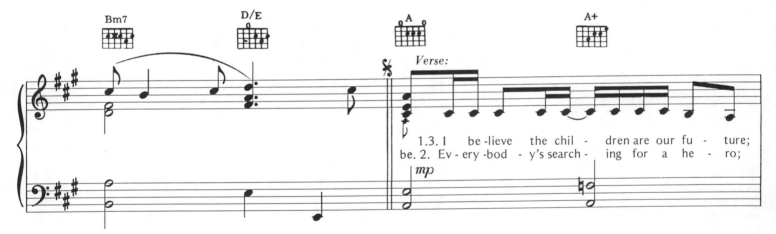

1.3. I be-lieve the chil - dren are our fu - ture;
be. 2. Ev - ery - bod - y's search - ing for a he - ro;

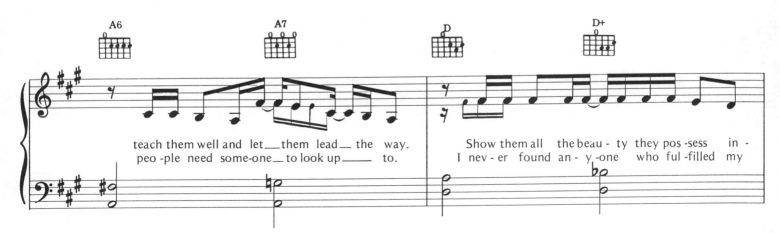

teach them well and let___ them lead___ the way.
peo - ple need some - one___ to look up___ to.

Show them all the beau - ty they pos - sess in
I nev - er found an - y - one who ful - filled my

The Greatest Love of All - 4 - 1

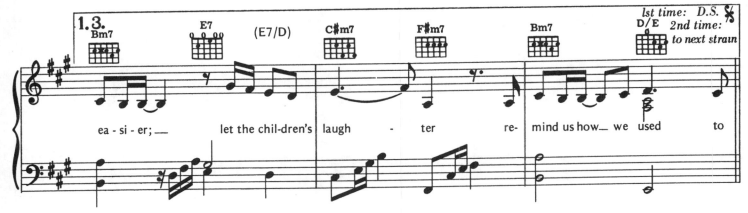

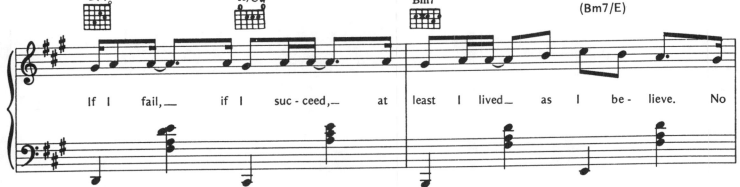

Chorus:

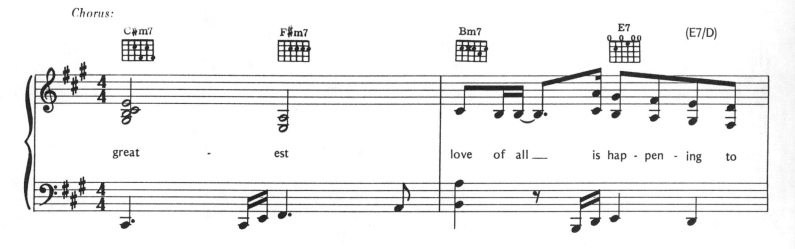

great - est   love of all __ is hap-pen-ing to

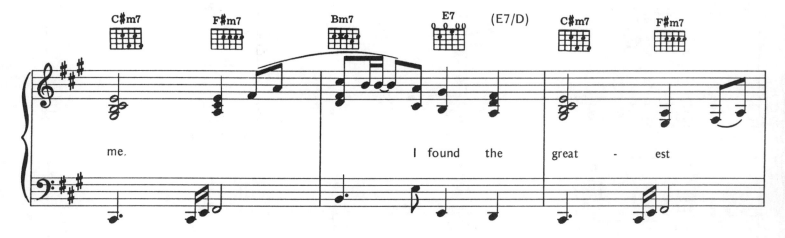

me.   I found the   great - est

love of all __ in -side   of   me. The great - est   love _____ of all

cresc.   *f*

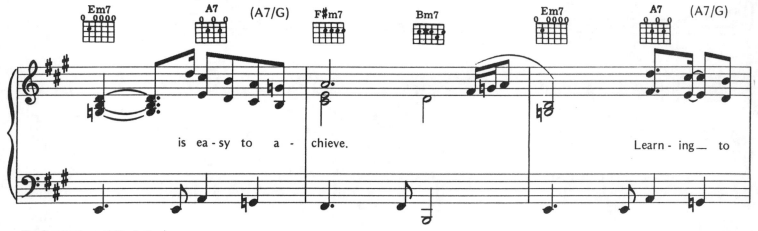

is ea - sy to a - chieve.   Learn - ing __ to

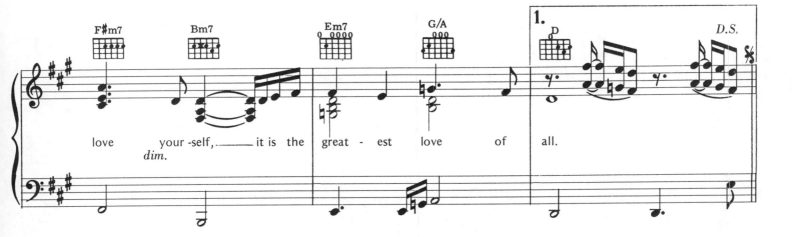

love your-self, ____ it is the great-est love of all.

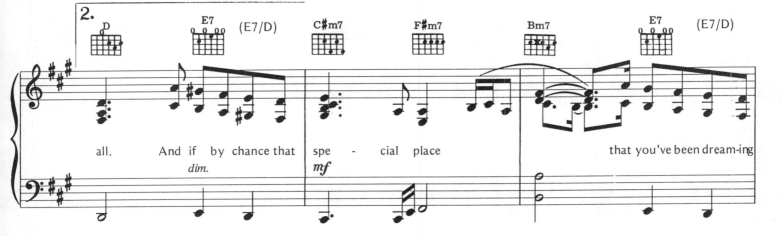

all. And if by chance that spe - cial place that you've been dream-ing

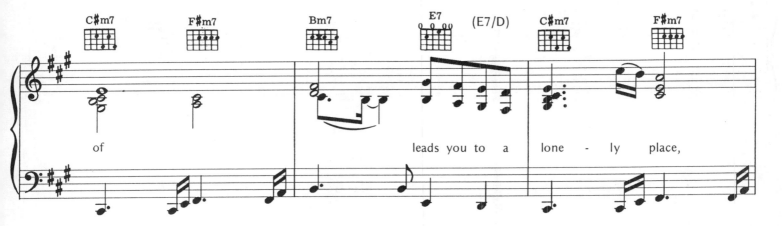

of leads you to a lone - ly place,

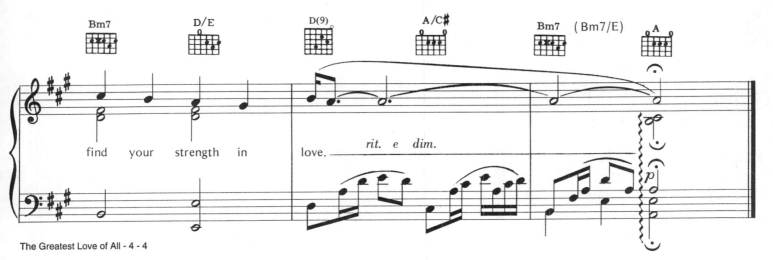

find your strength in love. ____ *rit. e dim.*

HANDS

Words and Music by
JEWEL KILCHER and PATRICK LEONARD

Hands - 5 - 1

Verse 2:
Poverty stole your golden shoes,
It didn't steal your laughter.
And heartache came to visit me,
But I knew it wasn't ever after.
We'll fight not out of spite,
For someone must stand up for what's right.
'Cause where there's a man who has no voice,
There ours shall go on singing.
(To Chorus:)

HOTEL CALIFORNIA

Words and Music by
DON FELDER, DON HENLEY
and GLENN FREY

Moderate Rock beat

On a dark des-ert high - way, cool wind in my
Her mind is Tif - fa - ny twist - ed. She got the Mer - ce - des

Hotel California - 7 - 1

Hotel California - 7 - 5

126

Hotel California - 7 - 7

HERO

By
WALTER AFANASIEFF and MARIAH CAREY

Moderate ballad

Hero - 4 - 1

129

Hero - 4 - 2

From the Touchstone Motion Picture "CON AIR"

HOW DO I LIVE

Words and Music by
DIANE WARREN

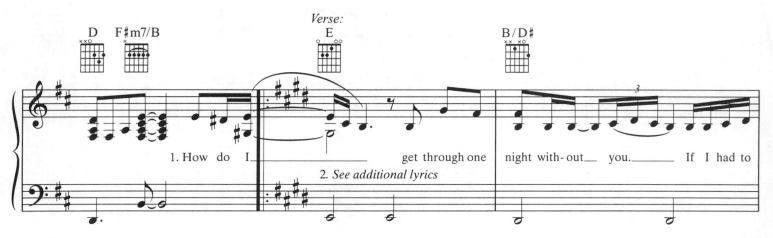

How Do I Live - 4 - 1

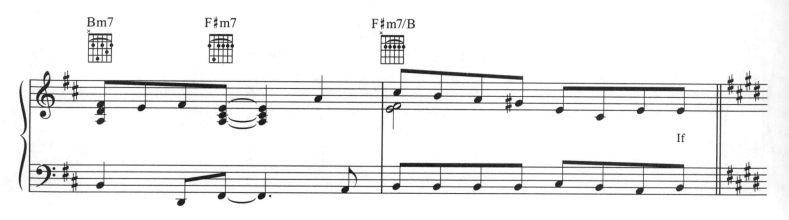

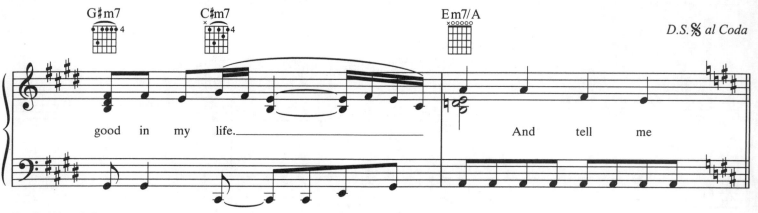

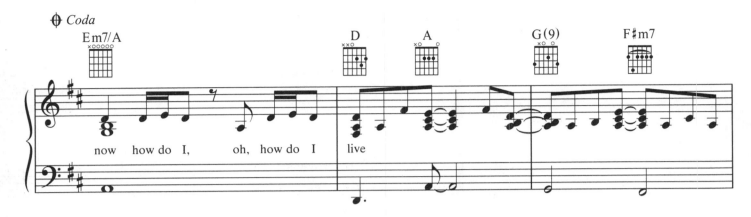

now how do I, oh, how do I live

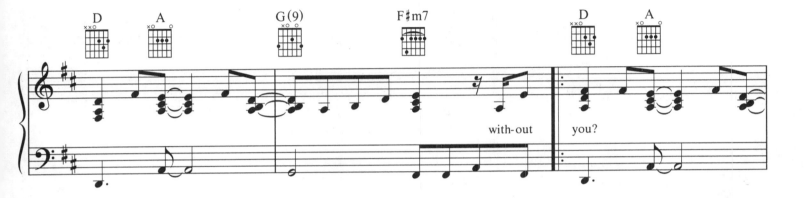

with-out you?

Repeat ad lib. and fade
(vocal 1st time only)

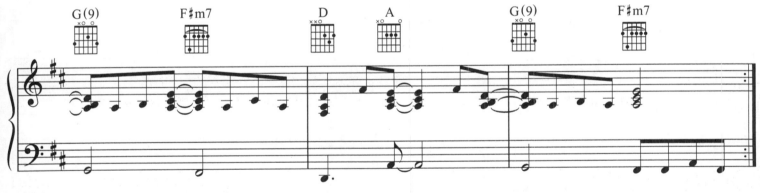

Verse 2:
Without you, there'd be no sun in my sky,
There would be no love in my life,
There'd be no world left for me.
And I, baby, I don't know what I would do,
I'd be lost if I lost you.
If you ever leave,
Baby, you would take away everything real in my life.
And tell me now...
(To Chorus:)

I BELIEVE I CAN FLY

Words and Music by
R. KELLY

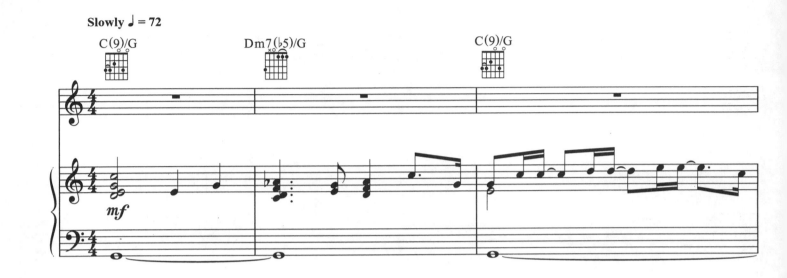

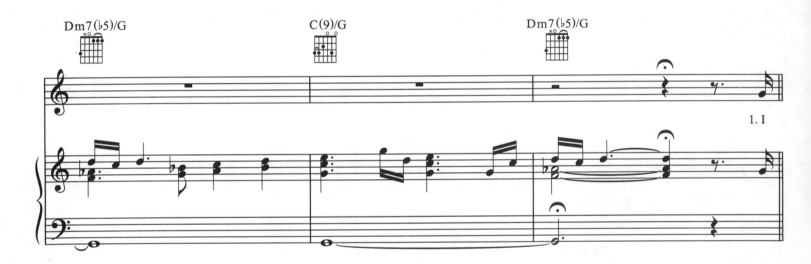

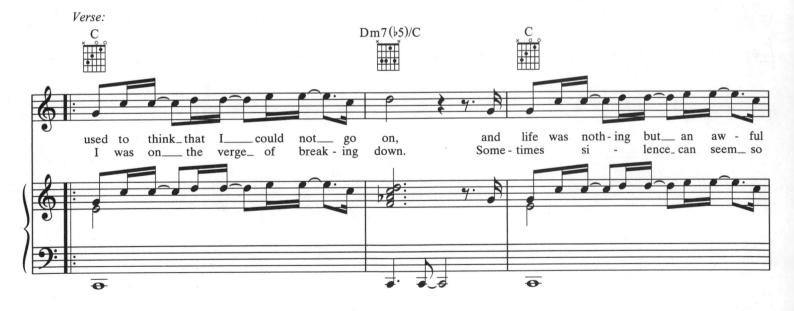

used to think_ that I___ could not__ go on, and life was noth - ing but__ an aw - ful
I was on___ the verge_ of break - ing down. Some - times si - lence_ can seem__ so

I Believe I Can Fly - 5 - 1

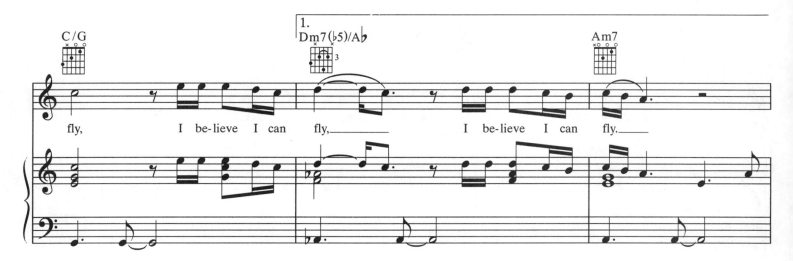

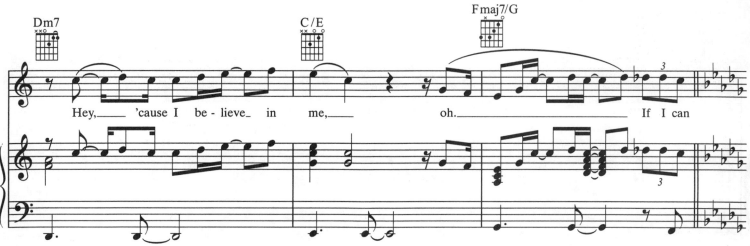

I Believe I Can Fly - 5 - 3

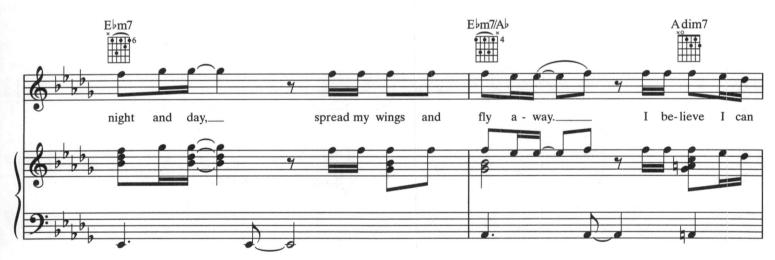

I Believe I Can Fly - 5 - 4

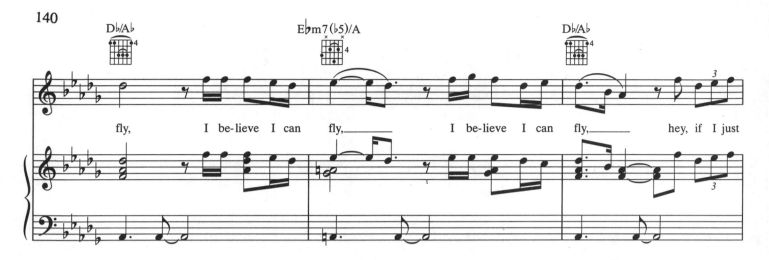

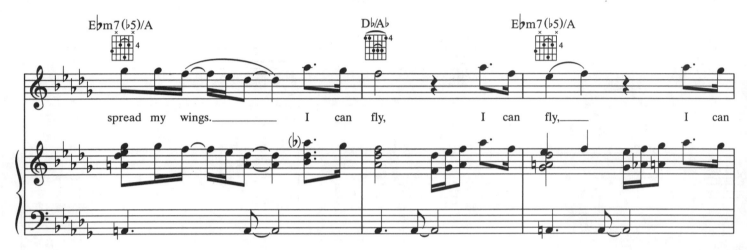

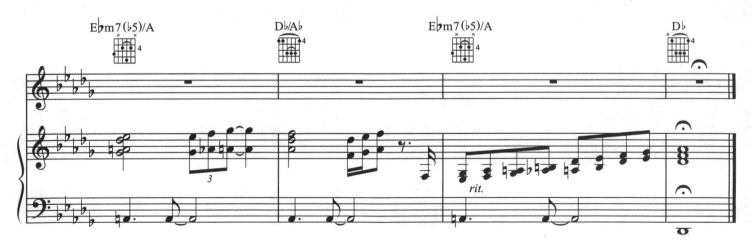

I CROSS MY HEART

Words and Music by
STEVE DORFF and ERIC KAZ

I Cross My Heart - 5 - 1

From here — on af - ter — let's stay the way we are — right — now.

— And share all the love — and laugh - ter — that a

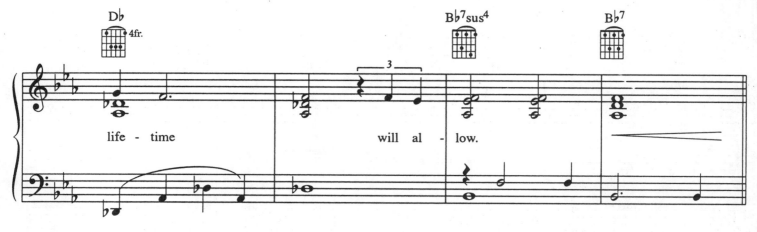

life - time will al - low.

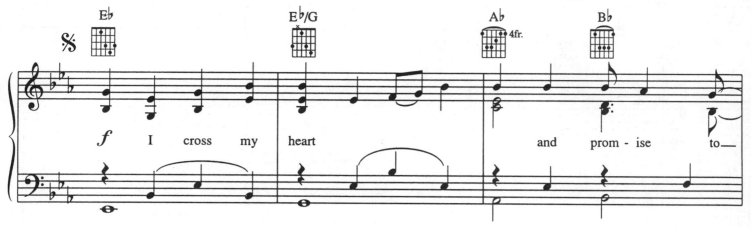

𝆑 I cross my heart and prom - ise to —

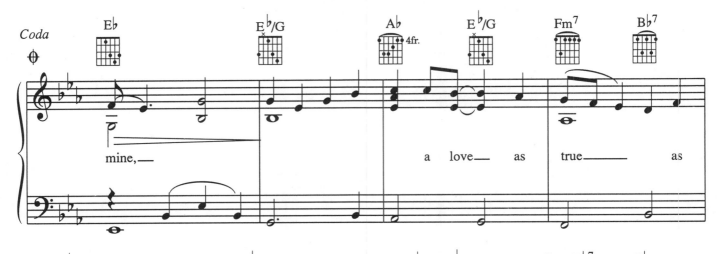

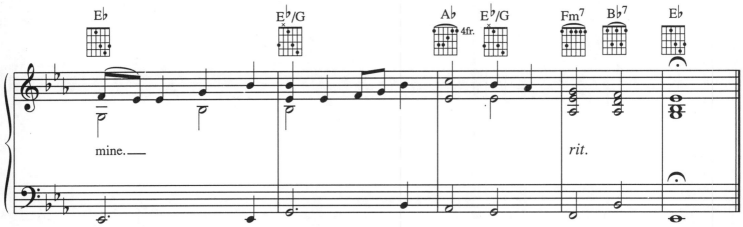

Additional Lyrics

2. You will always be the miracle
   That makes my life complete.
   And as long as there's a breath in me
   I'll make yours just as sweet.
   As we look into the future,
   It's as far as we can see.
   So let's make each tomorrow
   Be the best that it can be.
   (To Chorus)

I COULD NOT ASK FOR MORE

Words and Music by
DIANE WARREN

I Could Not Ask for More - 4 - 2

Chorus:

more_ than this time to - geth - er. I could not ask for more than this time with you.__ Ev - 'ry

prayer I have's_ been an-swered and ev - 'ry dream I have's_come true.__ And

right here in this mo-ment is right where I'm meant to be.__ Oh, here with_ you, here with__

me,_____ oh._____

I DO (CHERISH YOU)

Words and Music by
KEITH STEGALL and DAN HILL

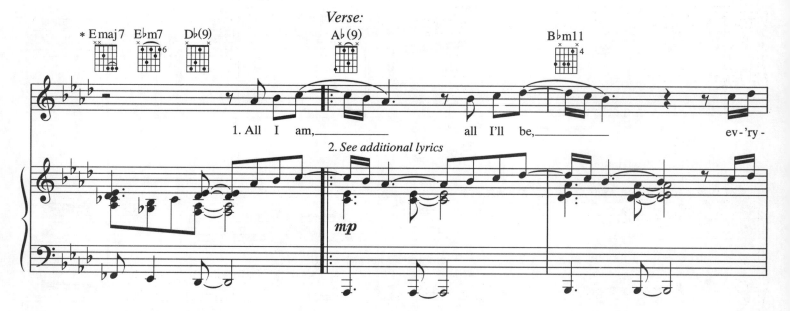

*Enharmonic chord labeling of F♭maj7.

I Do (Cherish You) - 5 - 1

ask-ing do I love you this much,___ well, ba - by, I do.___

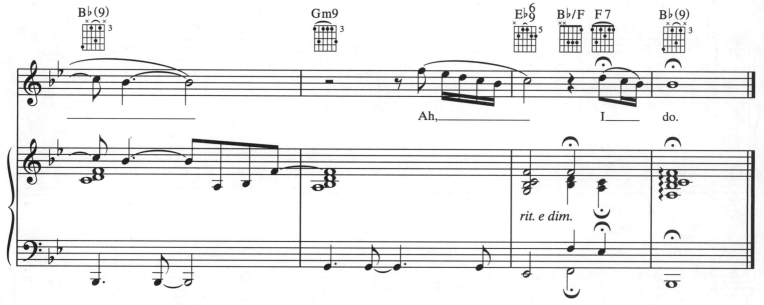

Ah,___ I___ do.

rit. e dim.

Verse 2:
In my world before you,
I lived outside my emotions.
Didn't know where I was going
Till that day I found you.
How you opened my life
To a new paradise.
In a world torn by change,
Still with all of my heart,
Till my dying day . . .
(To Chorus:)

From Touchstone Pictures' ARMAGEDDON

I DON'T WANT TO MISS A THING

Words and Music by
DIANE WARREN

I Don't Want to Miss a Thing - 7 - 1

160

Repeat ad lib. and fade

From the Motion Picture "Robin Hood: Prince Of Thieves"

(EVERYTHING I DO) I DO IT FOR YOU

Lyrics and Music by
BRYAN ADAMS, ROBERT JOHN LANGE
and MICHAEL KAMEN

Look in-to my eyes,— you will see—
Look in-to your heart,— you will find— there's

what you mean to — me. Search your heart,— search your
noth - ing there to — hide. So, take me as I am, take my

(Everything I Do) I Do It for You - 4 - 1

I LOVE YOU ALWAYS FOREVER

Words and Music by
DONNA LEWIS

"I Love You Always Forever" is inspired by the H.E. Bates novel *"Love for Lydia."*
Chorus/Bridge lyric courtesy of *Michael Joseph Ltd.* and *The Estate of H.E. Bates.*

168

I Love You Always Forever - 5 - 3

I love you, al - ways for-ev-er, near and far, clos - er to-geth - er.

Ev - ery-where, I__ will be with you, ev-ery-thing, I__ will do for you. I love you, al - ways for-ev-er,

near and far, clo - ser to-geth - er. Ev - ery-where, I__ will be with you, ev - ery-thing, I__ will do for you.

Repeat ad lib. and fade

I Love You Always Forever - 5 - 5

Verse 3:
You've got the most unbelievable blue eyes I've ever seen.
You've got me almost melting away as we lay there
Under blue sky with pure white stars,
Exotic sweetness, a magical time.
(To Chorus:)

I WANT IT THAT WAY

Words and Music by
MAX MARTIN and
ANDREAS CARLSSON

I Want It That Way - 5 - 1

172

I Want It That Way - 5 - 2

I SWEAR

By
GARY BAKER and FRANK MYERS

I Swear - 4 - 1

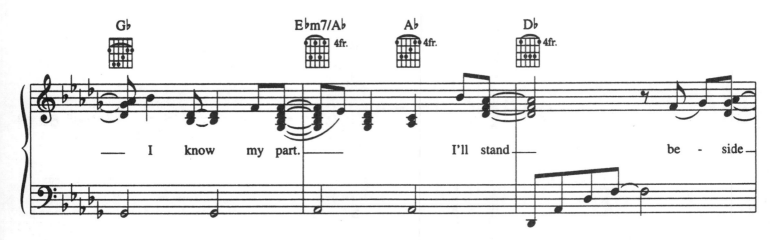

I know my part. I'll stand be- side

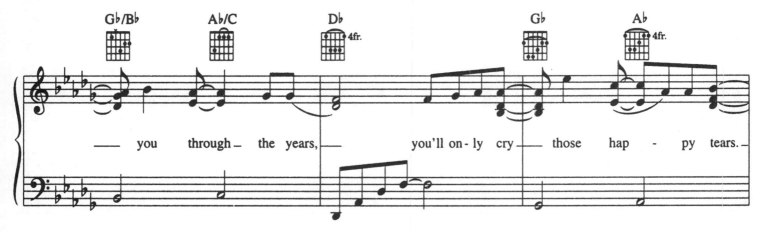

you through the years, you'll on-ly cry those hap-py tears.

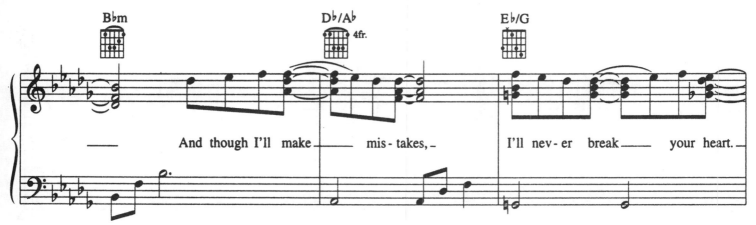

And though I'll make mis- takes, I'll nev-er break your heart.

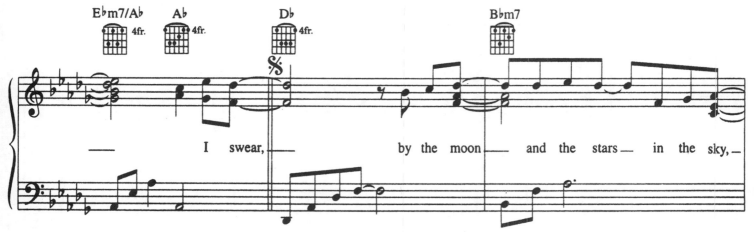

I swear, by the moon and the stars in the sky,

178

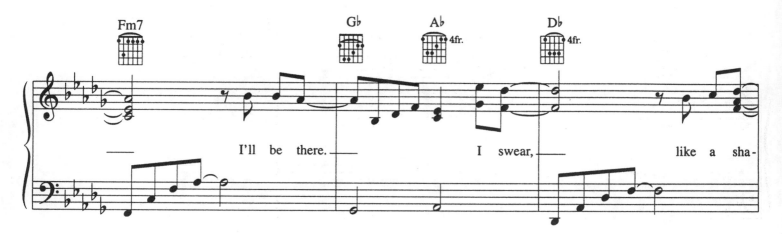

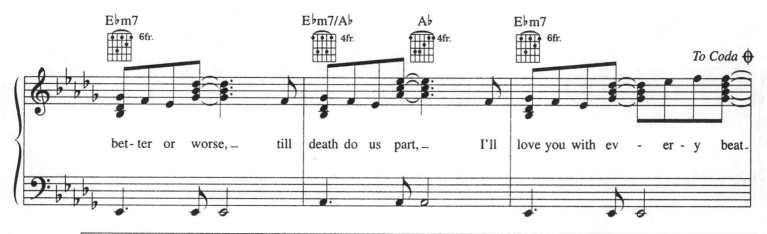

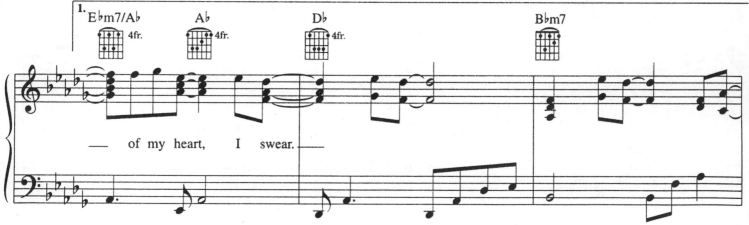

I Swear - 4 - 3

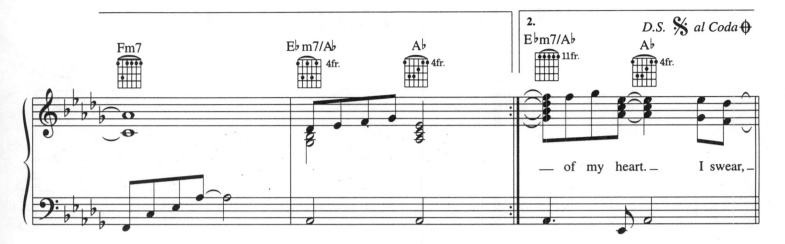

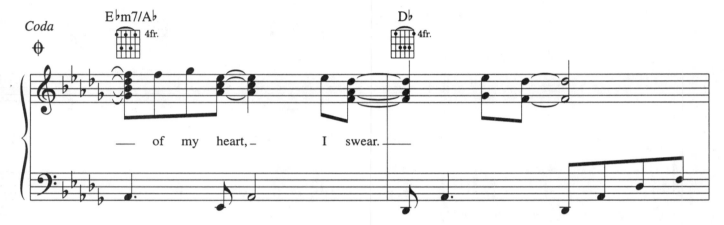

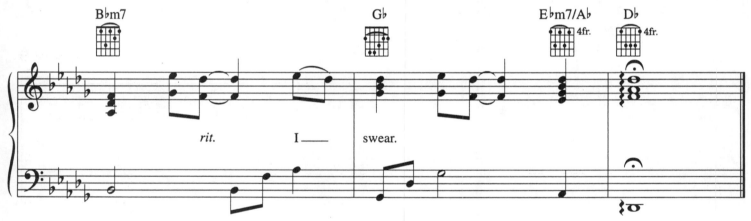

Additional lyrics

2. I'll give you everything I can,
I'll build your dreams with these two hands,
And we'll hang some memories on the wall.
And when there's silver in your hair,
You won't have to ask if I still care,
'Cause as time turns the page my love won't age at all.
(To Chorus)

I WILL ALWAYS LOVE YOU

Words and Music by
DOLLY PARTON

Moderately slow, with feeling ♩ = 69   *Verse 1:*

I Will Always Love You - 5 - 1

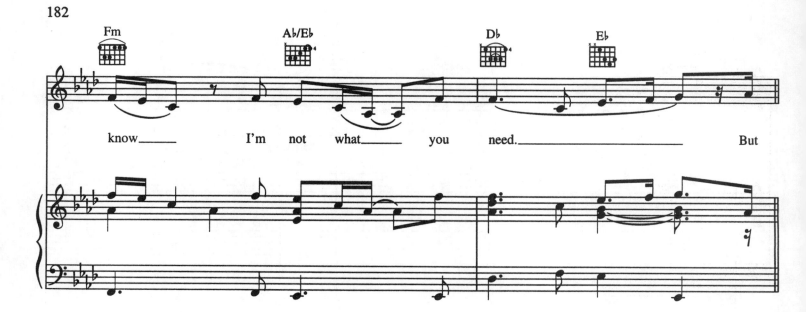

know_____ I'm not what_____ you need._____ But

Chorus:

I_____ will al - ways_ love___ you._____ I_____ will_

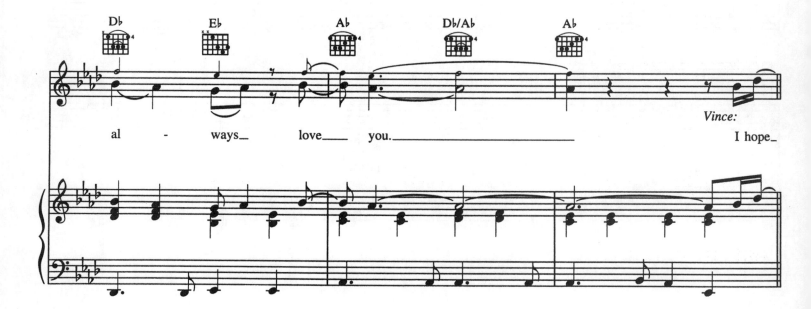

al - ways_ love___ you._____

Vince:

I hope_

Chorus:

Printed in USA

OOPS!... I DID IT AGAIN

Words and Music by
MAX MARTIN and RAMI

Oops!... I Did It Again - 7 - 1

188

Oops!… I Did It Again - 7 - 4

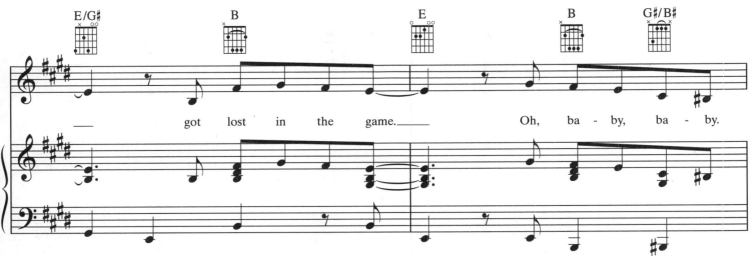

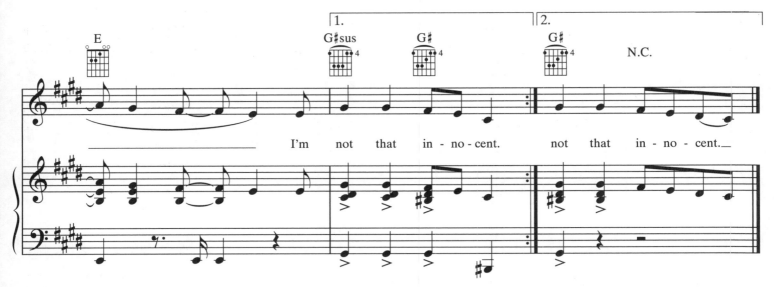

From The Fox Searchlight Film, "THE BROTHERS McMULLEN"

I WILL REMEMBER YOU

Words and Music by
SARAH McLACHLAN, SEAMUS EGAN
and DAVE MERENDA

I Will Remember You - 4 - 1

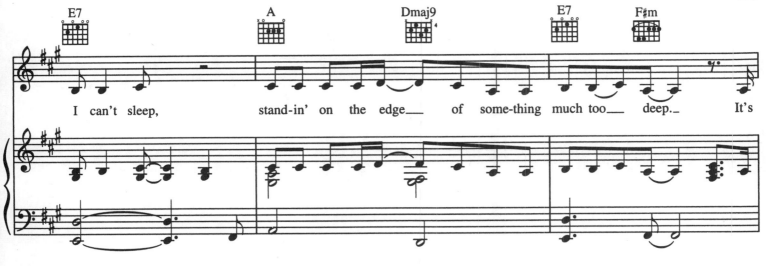

I can't sleep, stand-in' on the edge___ of some-thing much too___ deep.___ It's

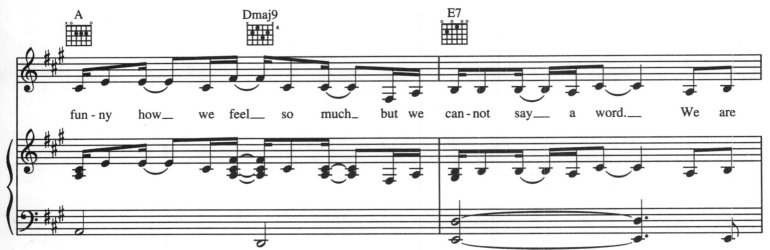

fun-ny how___ we feel___ so much___ but we can-not say___ a word.___ We are

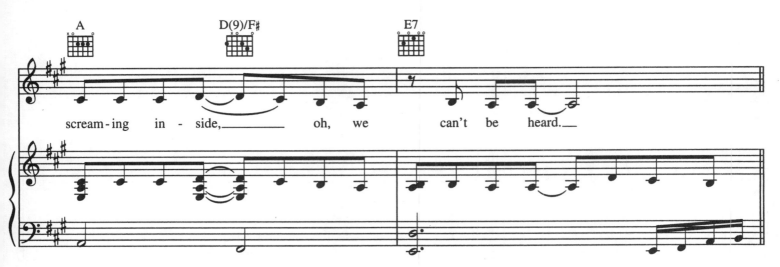

scream-ing in-side,_____ oh, we can't be heard.___

Chorus:

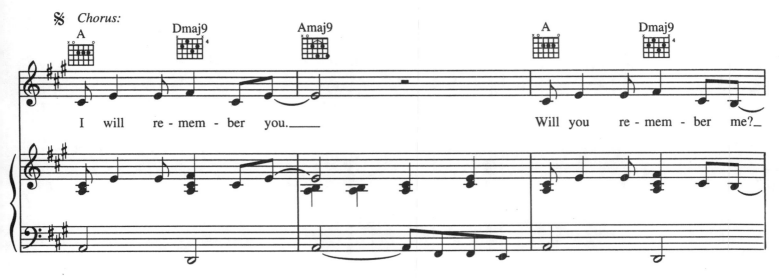

I will re-mem-ber you.___ Will you re-mem-ber me?___

Don't let your life___ pass___ you by,___

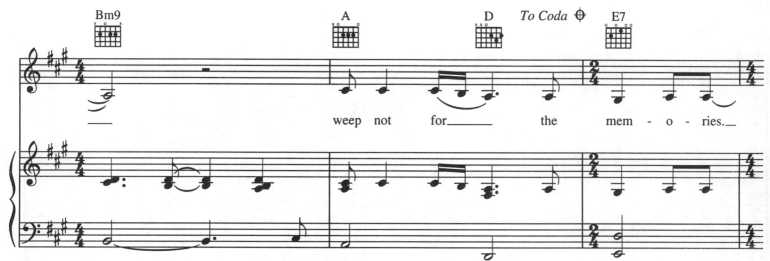

weep not for___ the mem - o - ries.

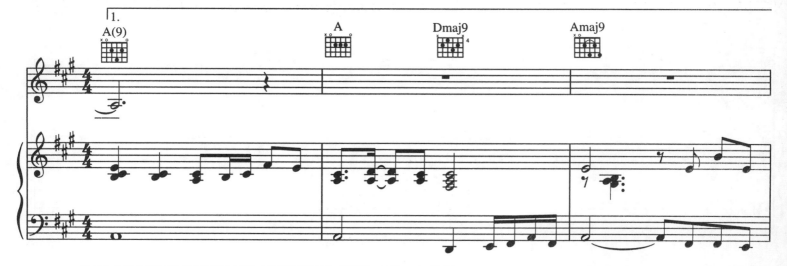

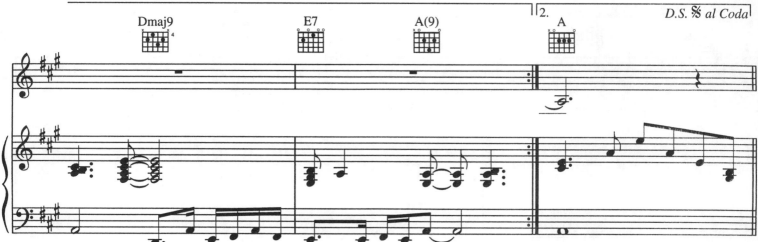

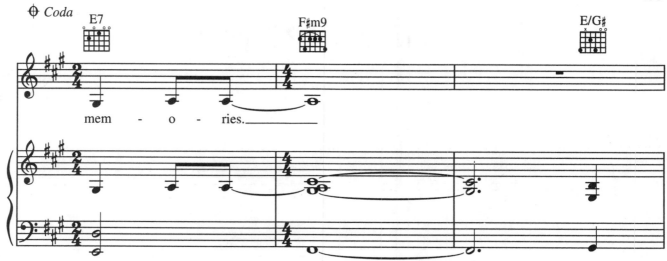

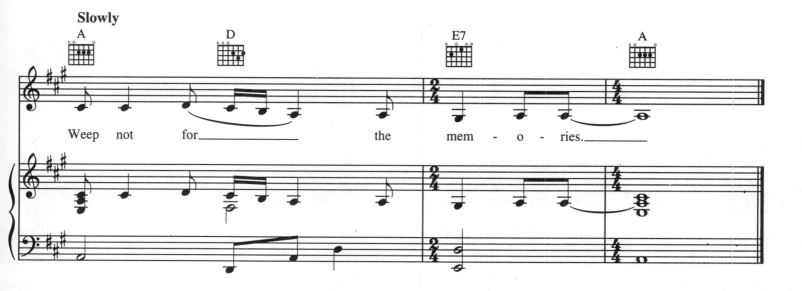

Verse 2:
So afraid to love you,
More afraid to lose.
I'm clinging to a past
That doesn't let me choose.
Where once there was a darkness,
A deep and endless night,
You gave me everything you had,
Oh, you gave me life.
(To Chorus:)

(Optional Verse 1 — Album version)
Remember the good times that we had,
I let them slip away from us when things got bad.
Now clearly I first saw you smiling in the sun.
I wanna feel your warmth upon me,
I wanna be the one.
(To Chorus:)

I'M YOUR ANGEL

Words and Music by
R. KELLY

Chorus:

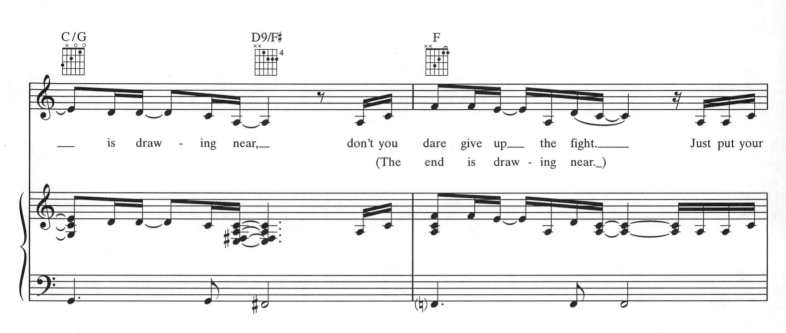

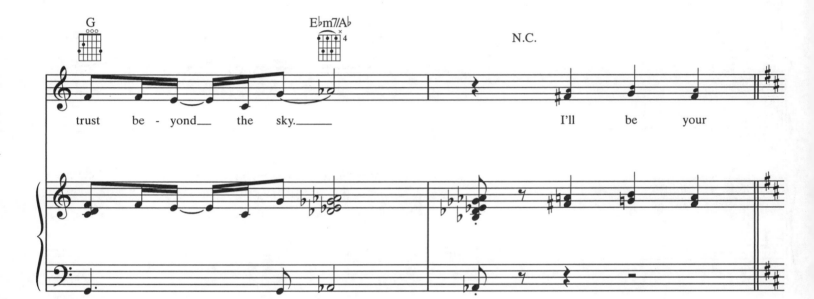

KISSING YOU
(Love Theme From "ROMEO + JULIET")

Words and Music by
DES'REE and TIM ATACK

Moderately slow ♩. = 112

1. Pride can stand a thou-sand tri-als, the strong will nev-er fall. But watch-ing stars with-out you, my soul cried.

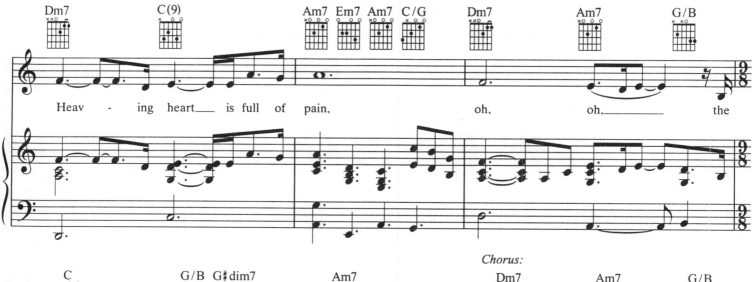

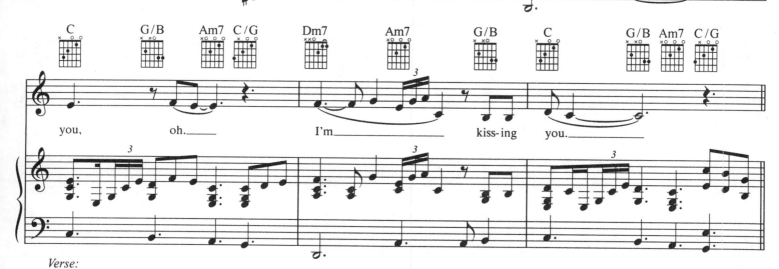

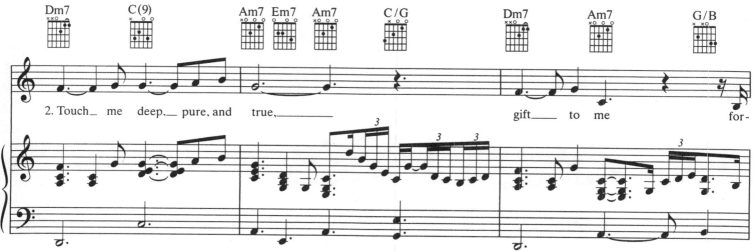

Chorus:

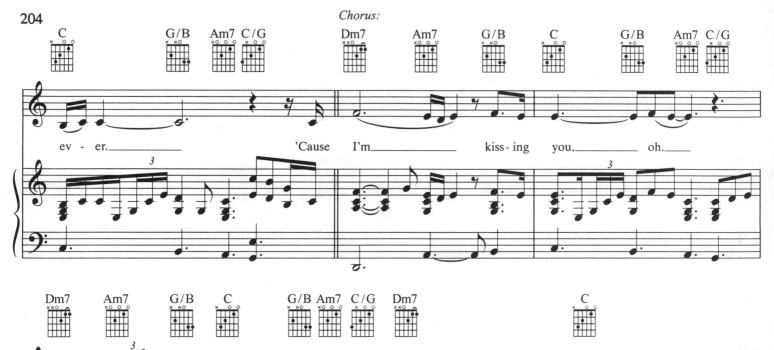

ev - er._____ 'Cause I'm_____ kiss- ing you,_____ oh.____

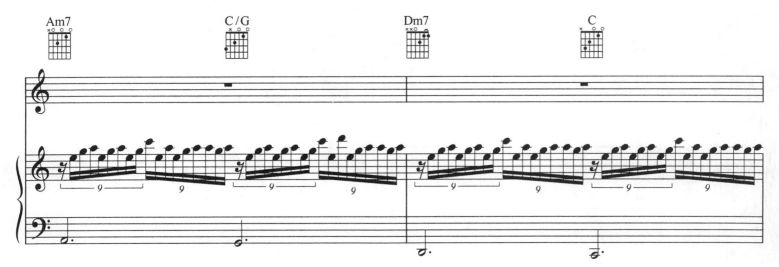

I'm_____ kiss- ing you._____

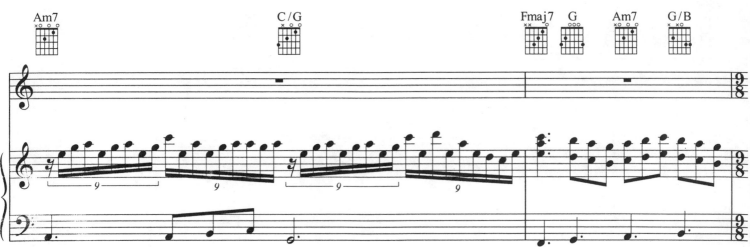

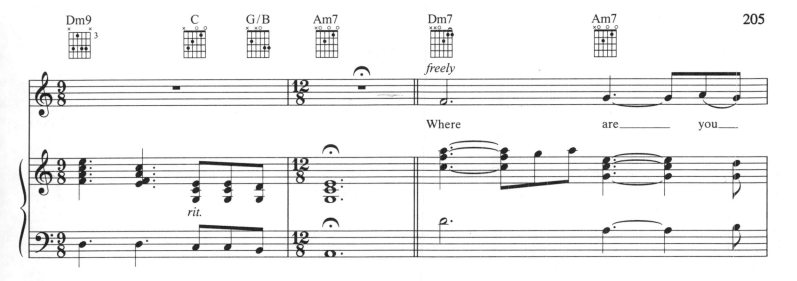

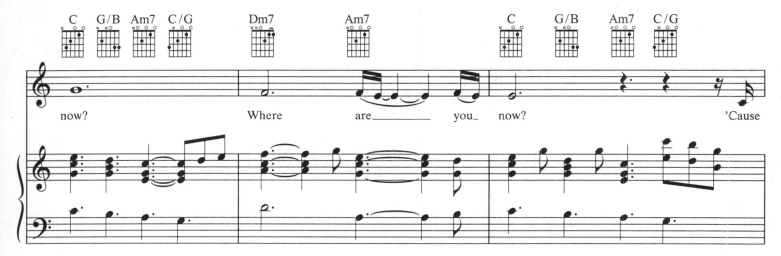

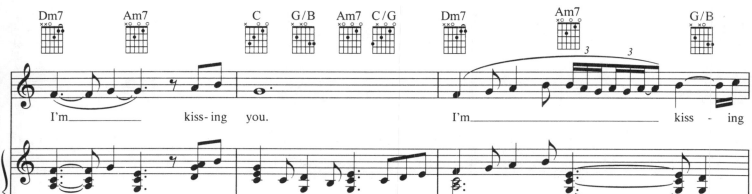

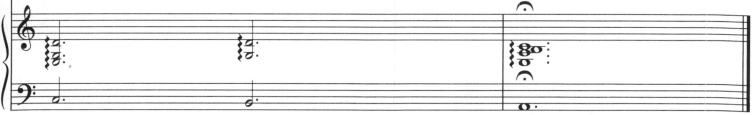

LARGER THAN LIFE

Words and Music by
MAX MARTIN, KRISTIAN LUNDIN
and BRIAN T. LITTRELL

Rock ♩ = 120

1. I may run and hide when you're scream-in' my name,____ al - right.____
2. Look - in' at the crowd and I see your bod - y sway,____ come on.____

Larger Than Life - 6 - 1

But let me tell you now there are
Wish-in' I could thank you in a

pric-es to fame,_ al-right._
dif-fer-ent way,_ come on._

All of_ our
'Cause all of_ your

time spent_ in flash-es_ of light..._
time spent_ keeps us_ a-live._

Chorus:

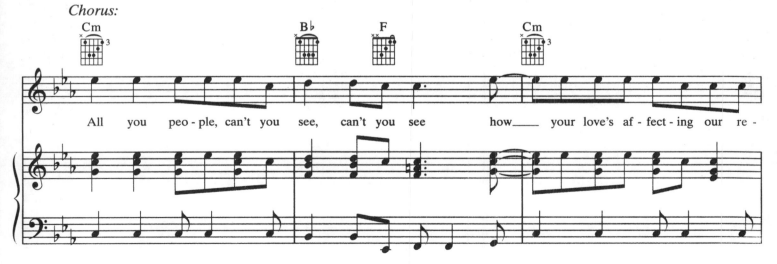

All you peo-ple, can't you see, can't you see how_ your love's af-fect-ing our re-

al - i - ty?_____ Ev - 'ry time we're down, you___ can make it right and

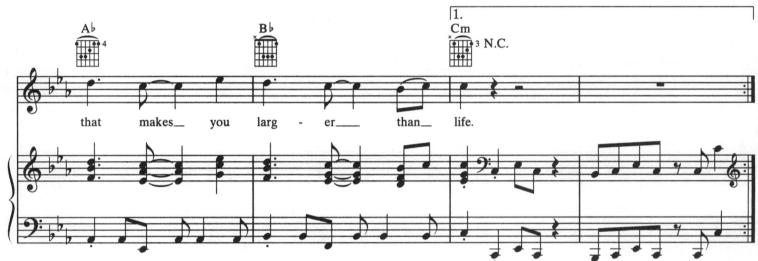

that makes__ you larg - er___ than__ life.

life.

Bridge:

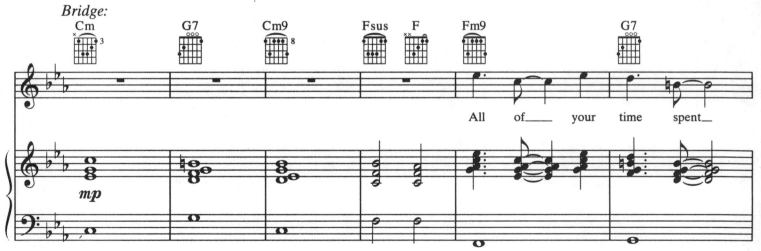

All of___ your time spent___

Larger Than Life - 6 - 4

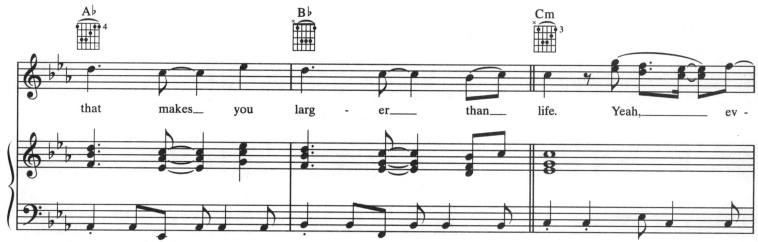

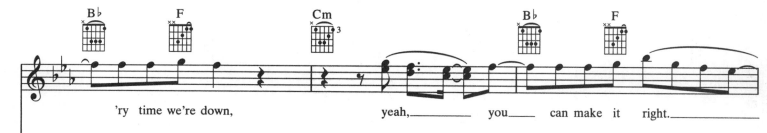

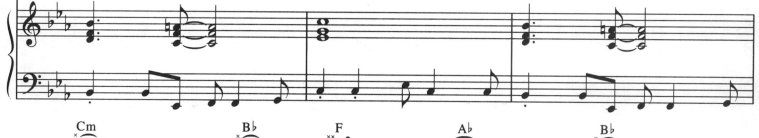

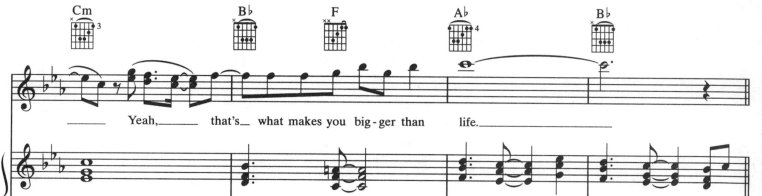

Larger Than Life - 6 - 5

Chorus:

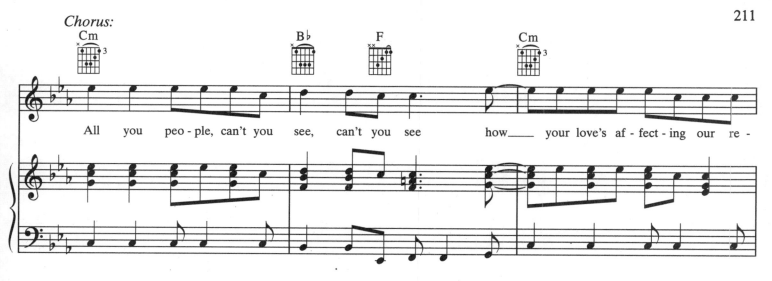

All you peo-ple, can't you see, can't you see how___ your love's af-fect-ing our re-

al - i - ty?_____ Ev - 'ry time we're down, you___ can make it right and

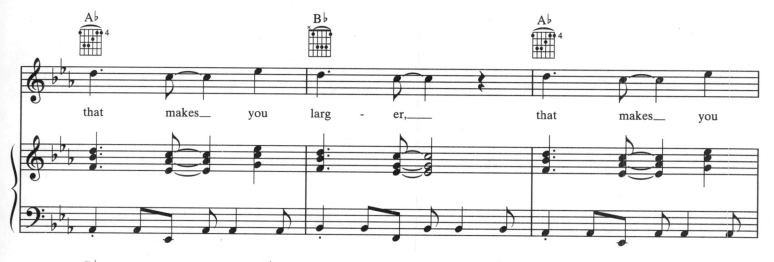

that makes___ you larg - er,___ that makes___ you

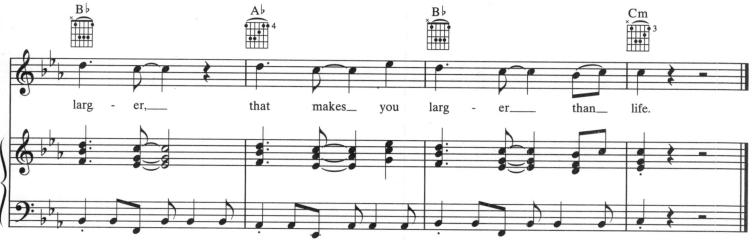

larg - er,___ that makes___ you larg - er___ than___ life.

LEAN ON ME

Words and Music by
BILL WITHERS

Moderately, with a beat

No chord

Some - times in our lives___
Please swal - low your pride___
If there is a load___

Lean on Me - 6 - 1

we all have pain,___ we all have sor - row.___
if I have things___ you need to bor - row,___
you have to bear___ that you can't car - ry,___

But if we are wise___ we know that there's___ al - ways to - mor -
for no one can fill___ those of your needs___ that you won't let___
I'm right up the road.___ I'll share your load___ if you just call___

-row.
show.} Lean on me___ when you're not strong___ and I'll be your friend.___
me.

C   Dm   Em   F   Em   Dm   C

214

Lean on Me - 6 - 3

Just call____ me a-when you need a friend.

Call____ me, oh, ba-by now. Call____ me a-when you need a friend.

1. Call____ me oh, ba-by now. 2. Call____ me ear-ly in the morn-in', now.

Repeat and fade

N.C.

(Spoken:) Pump it up, pump it up, pump it up, home boy, just like that.___

Lean on Me - 6 - 6

MORE THAN A FEELING

Words and Music by
TOM SCHOLZ

slips a - way.____

She slips a - way. _____

3. When I'm tired and thinking cold
   I hide in my music, forget the day
   And dream of a girl I used to know
   I closed my eyes and she slipped away.

(To Chorus)

OPEN ARMS

Words and Music by
STEVE PERRY and JONATHAN CAIN

Verse 3:
Living without you; living alone,
This empty house seems so cold.

Verse 4:
Wanting to hold you, wanting you near;
How much I wanted you home.

Bridge:
But now that you've come back;
Turned night into day;
I need you to stay.
(Chorus)

MORE THAN WORDS

Lyrics and Music by
BETTENCOURT, CHERONE

Moderate rock ♩ = 92

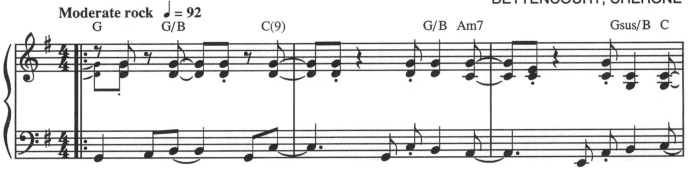

1. Say-in', "I___ love___ you" is not the words_ I want___ _ to___ hear_ from you.___ It's not that I___ want___ you not to say.___ But if_

_ you_ on-ly_ knew___ how_ eas - y___ it would be___ to___ show___

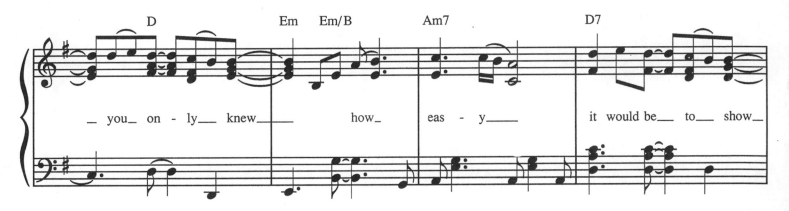

More Than Words - 4 - 1

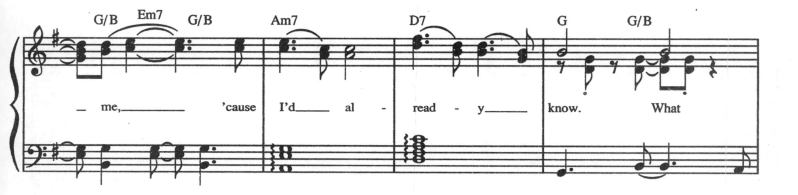

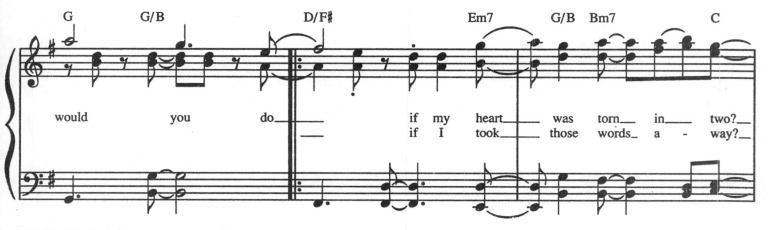

More than words_____ to show_ you feel_____ that your love_____ for me_ is_ real.
Then, you could - n't make_ things new_____ just by say -

What would you say_ - in' "I_ love_ you." - in' "I_ love_ you."

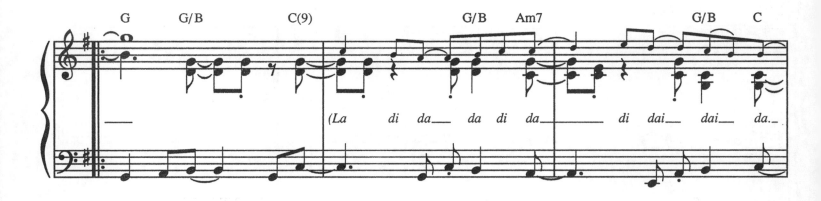

(La di da__ da di da_____ di dai_ dai_ da._

__) More_ than_ words.__ La di da__ da di da. _)

Verse 2:
Now that I have tried to talk to you
And make you understand.
All you have to do is close your eyes
And just reach out your hands.
And touch me, hold me close, don't ever let me go.
More than words is all I ever needed you to show.
Then you wouldn't have to say
That you love me 'cause I'd already know.
(To Chorus:)

From the Miramax Motion Picture "Music Of The Heart"

MUSIC OF MY HEART

Words and Music by
DIANE WARREN

done for my__ soul._____ You'll nev - er know__ the gift__ you've__
see - ing me__ through._____ You were the song__ that al - ways__

__ giv - en me._____ I'll car - ry it with me._____
__ made me sing._____ I'm sing - ing this for you._____

Through the days__ a - head,__ I think__ of days__ be - fore,__ when you made me
Ev - 'ry - where__ I go,__ I think__ of where__ I've been__ and of the

Chorus:

MY WAY

Original French Words by
GILES THIBAULT

English Words by PAUL ANKA
Music by JACQUES REVAUX
and CLAUDE FRANCOIS

My Way - 4 - 1

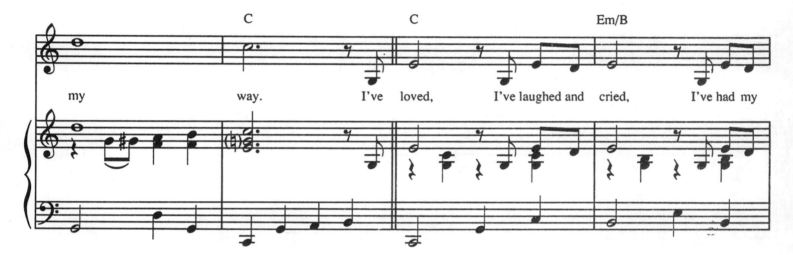

My Way - 4 - 4

NOW AND FOREVER

Words and Music by
RICHARD MARX

Now and Forever - 4 - 1

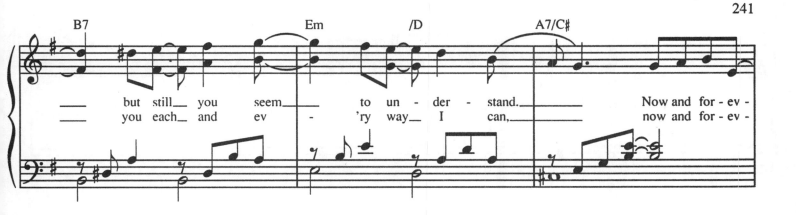

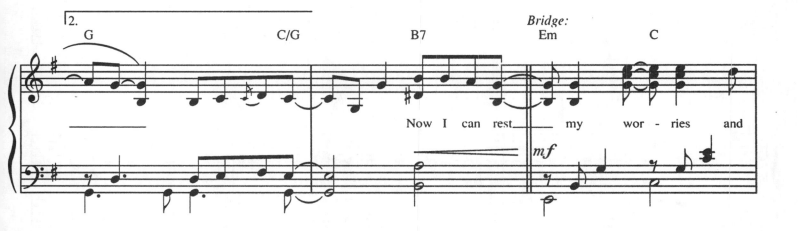

If I'd on-ly known___ you were there___ all the time,___ all this time.___

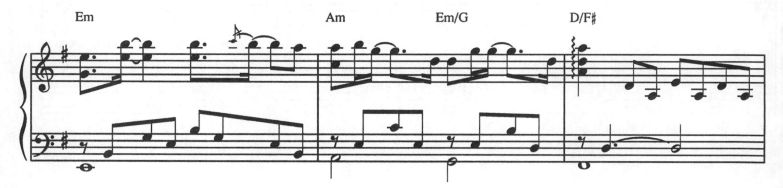

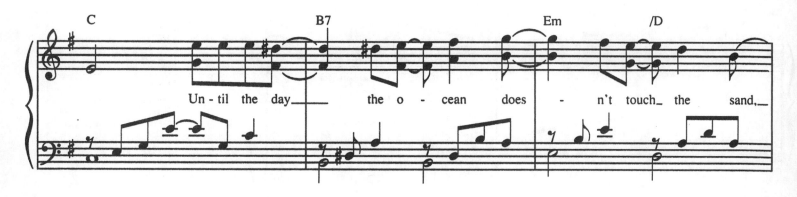

Un-til the day___ the o-cean does- -n't touch___ the sand,___

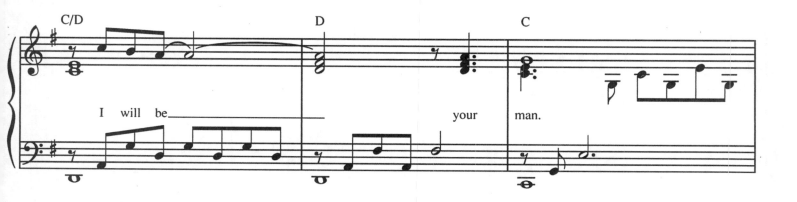

From the Motion Picture "THE WIZARD OF OZ"

OVER THE RAINBOW

Lyric by
E.Y. HARBURG

Music by
HAROLD ARLEN

When all the world is a hope-less jum-ble and the rain-drops tum-ble all a-round,

heav — en o-pens a mag-ic lane.

When all the clouds dark-en up the sky-way, there's a rain-bow high-way to be found,

Over the Rainbow - 4 - 1

Theme Song from the Mirisch-G&E Production "THE PINK PANTHER," a United Artists Release

THE PINK PANTHER

Music by
HENRY MANCINI

Moderately Mysterioso

The Pink Panther - 2 - 1

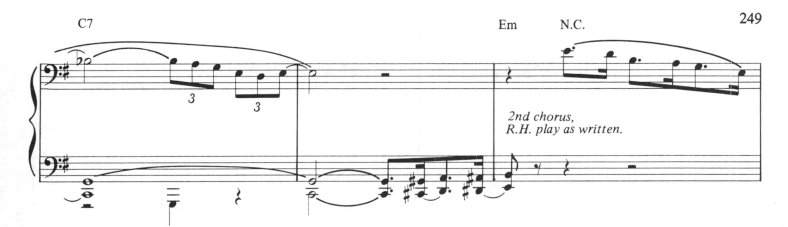

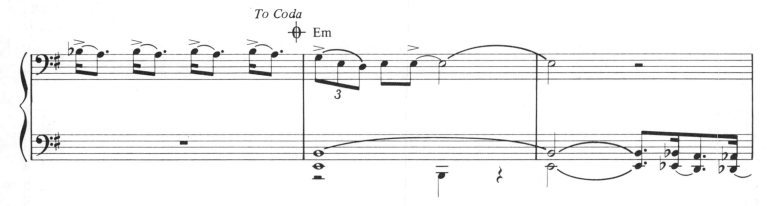

2nd chorus,
R.H. play as written.

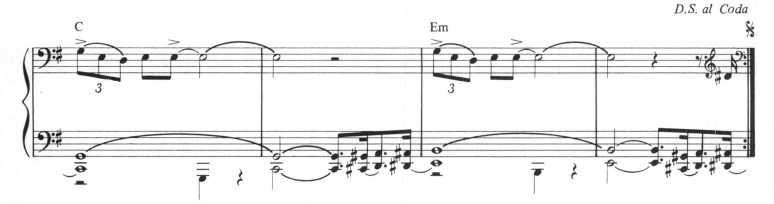

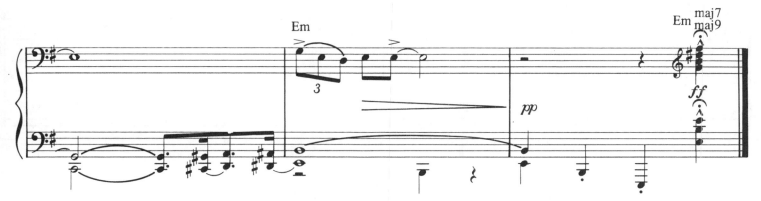

PLEASE FORGIVE ME

Words and Music by
BRYAN ADAMS
and ROBERT JOHN "MUTT" LANGE

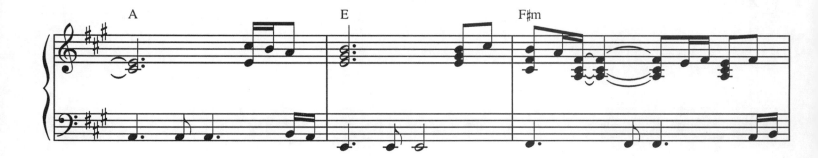

1. It still feels like_ our first night to-geth - er.___

Feels like the first__ kiss and it's get - tin' bet - ter, ba - by.

Please Forgive Me - 6 - 1

No one can bet - ter this.__ We're still hold - in' on,__ you're still the

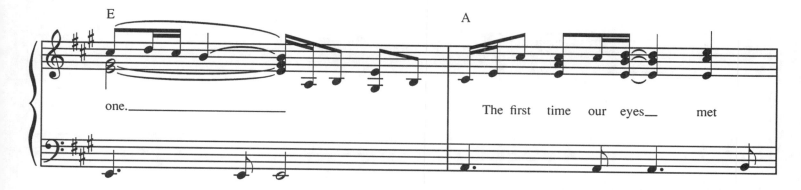

one.__ The first time our eyes__ met

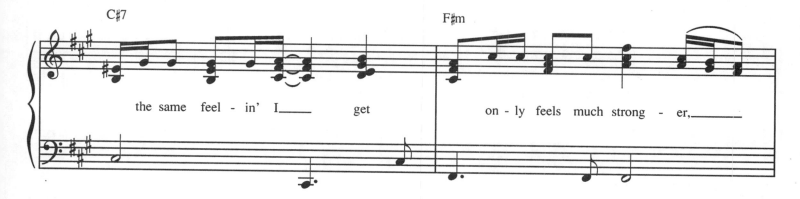

the same feel - in' I__ get on - ly feels much strong - er,__

and I wan - na love you long - er.__ You still turn the fire__ on.__

__ So, if you're feel - in' lone - ly, don't.__

mf

You're the on - ly one__ I'll ev - er want._____ I on - ly

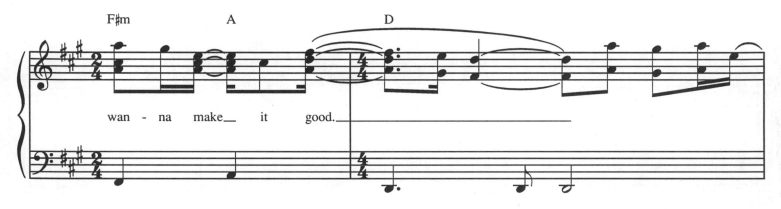

wan - na make__ it good._____

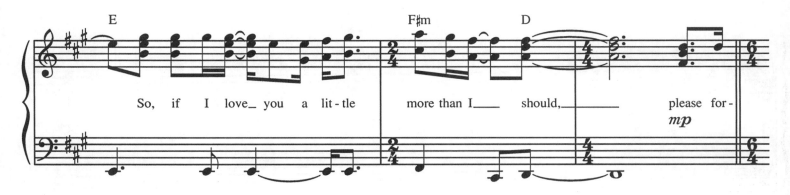

So, if I love_ you a lit - tle more than I___ should,_____ please for-
mp

Chorus:

give me,__ I know not what I do.__ Please for - give me,__ I can't stop lov - in' you.__ Don't de-

ny me__ this pain I'm go - in' through._Please for - give me,__ if I need you like I do.__ {Please / Oh,} be-
mf

lieve me,____ ev-'ry word I say is true.__ Please for-give me,____ I can't stop lov-in' you.__

2. It still

feels like_ our best times_ are to-geth-give me,____ I can't stop lov-in' you.__

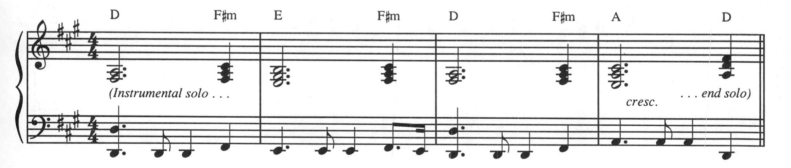

(Instrumental solo . . .   cresc.   . . . end solo)

Bridge:

The one thing I'm sure____ of   is the way we make____ love.

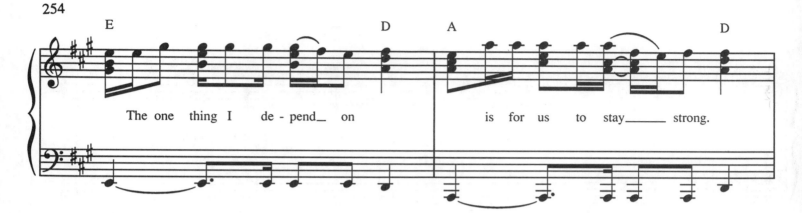

give me,___ if I can't stop lov-in' you.___ Now,___ be - lieve_ me,___ I don't know what I'd do.___ Please for-

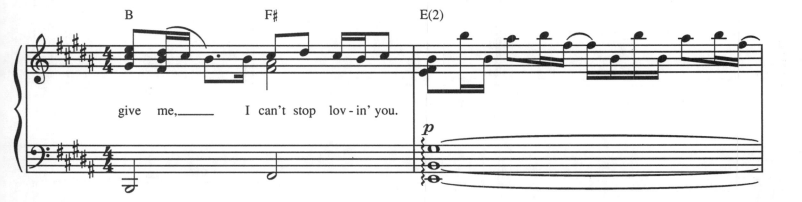

give me,_____ I can't stop lov - in' you.

Can't stop lov - in' you.

rit.

Verse 2:
It still feels like our best times are together.
Feels like the first touch, we're still gettin' closer, baby.
Can't get close enough.
We're still holdin' on, you're still number one.
I remember the smell of your skin, I remember everything.
I remember all your moves, I remember you, yeah.
I remember the nights, you know I still do.
So, if you're feelin' lonely, don't.
You're the only one I'll ever want.
I only wanna make it good.
So, if I love you a little more than I should, . . .
(To Chorus:)

THE PRAYER

Italian Lyric by
ALBERTO TESTA and TONY RENIS

Words and Music by
CAROLE BAYER SAGER and DAVID FOSTER

to a place where we'll be safe.

Male:

La lu-ce che tu

Verse 2:

I pray we'll find your light,

and hold it in our

dai,

nel cuo-re res-te-rá.

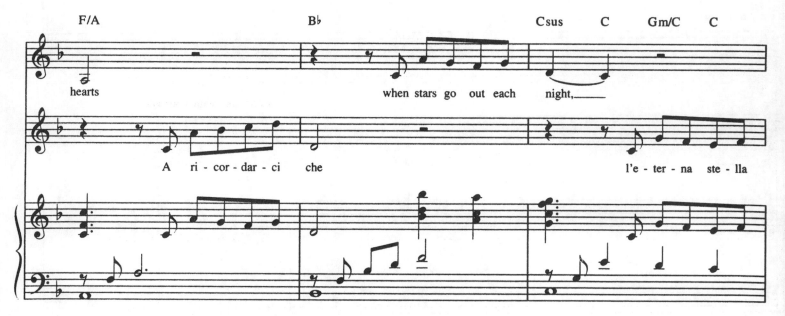

hearts

when stars go out each night,____

A ri-cor-dar-ci che

l'e-ter-na ste-lla

262

The Prayer - 8 - 7

From "MY BEST FRIEND'S WEDDING"

I SAY A LITTLE PRAYER

Words by
HAL DAVID

Music by
BURT BACHARACH

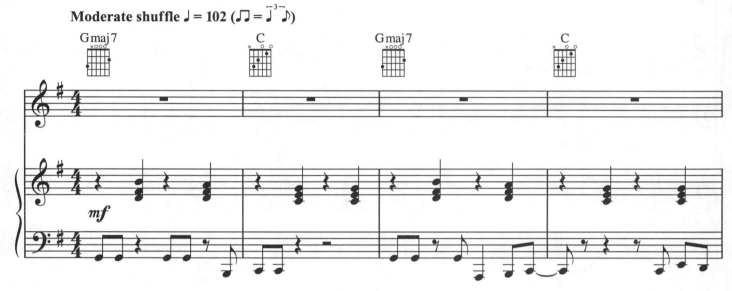

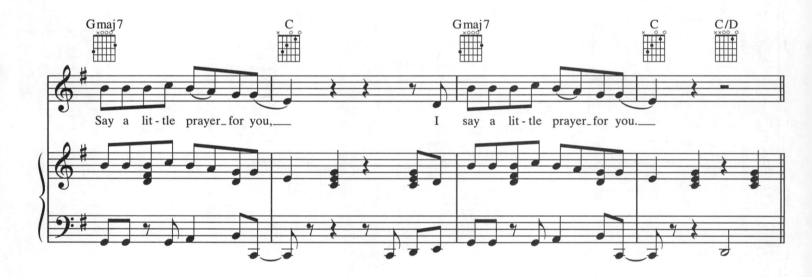

Say a lit-tle prayer for you,____ I say a lit-tle prayer for you.____

Verses 1 & 2:

1. The mo-ment I wake____ up,____ be-fore I put
2. I run____ for the bus,____ dear,____ while rid-ing I

I Say a Little Prayer - 6 - 1

Chorus:

I Say a Little Prayer - 6 - 6

RIGHT HERE WAITING

Words and Music by
RICHARD MARX

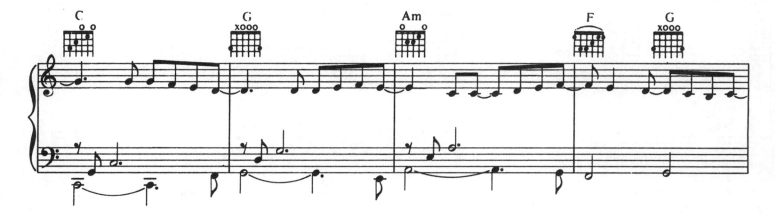

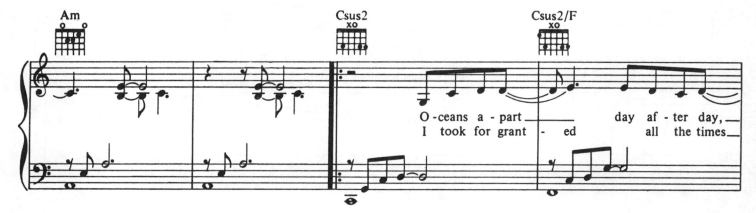

O-ceans a - part___ day af - ter day,___
I took for grant - ed all the times___

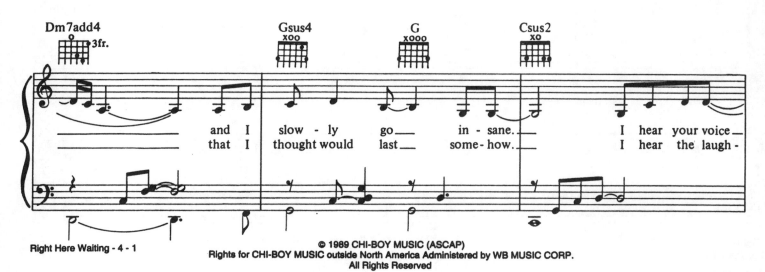

and I slow - ly go___ in - sane.___ I hear your voice___
that I thought would last___ some - how. I hear the laugh -

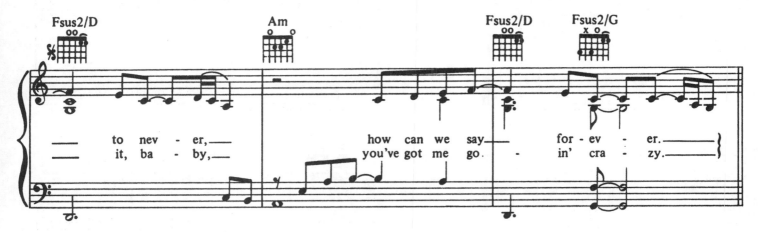

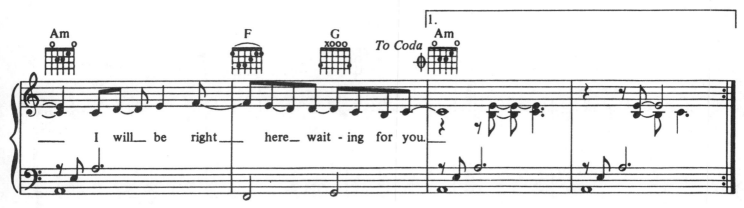

Right Here Waiting - 4 - 2

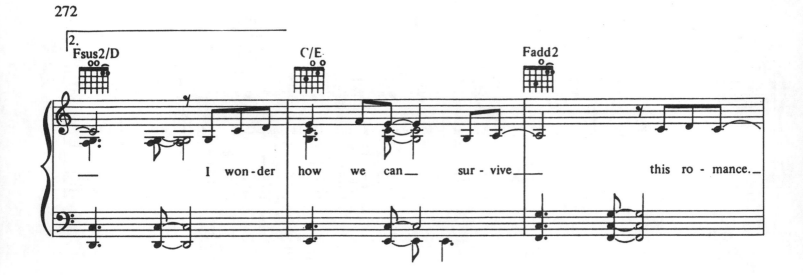

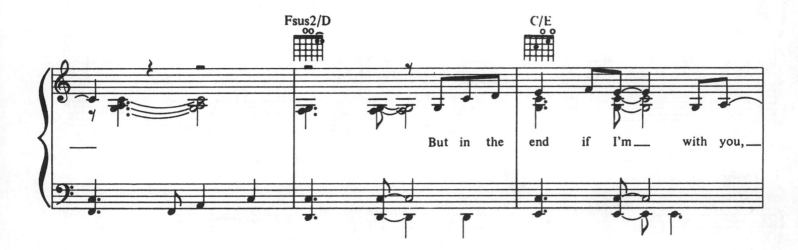

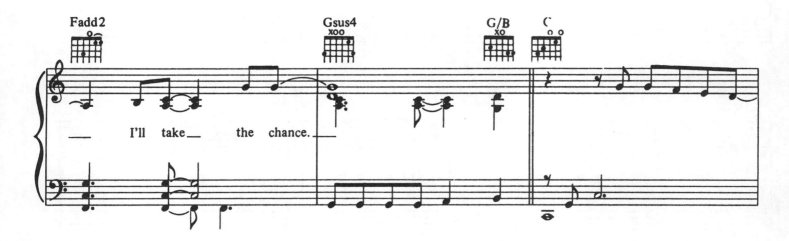

D.S. (lyric 2) al Coda

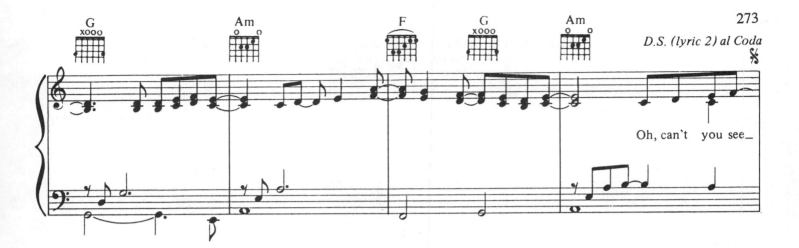

Oh, can't you see_

Coda

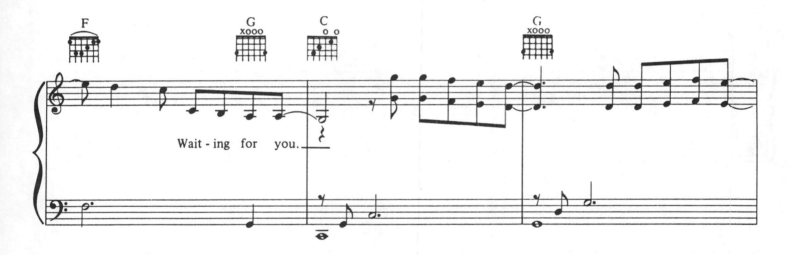

Wait - ing for you._

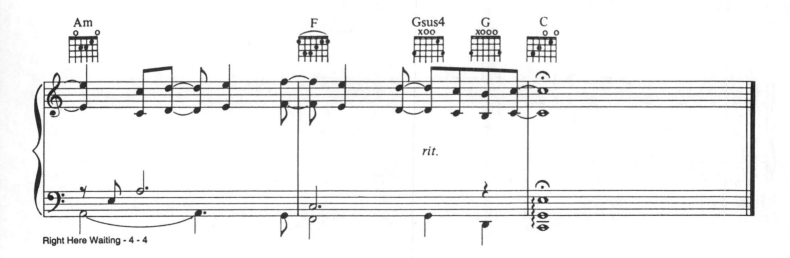

rit.

Right Here Waiting - 4 - 4

From the Twentieth Century-Fox Motion Picture "THE ROSE"

THE ROSE

Words and Music by
AMANDA McBROOM

love   it is a riv - er that drowns _____ the ten - der
love   it is a ra - zor that leaves _____ your soul to

1. _____ reed. Some - say _____ bleed.   Some say _____

2. Some say

The Rose - 4 - 1

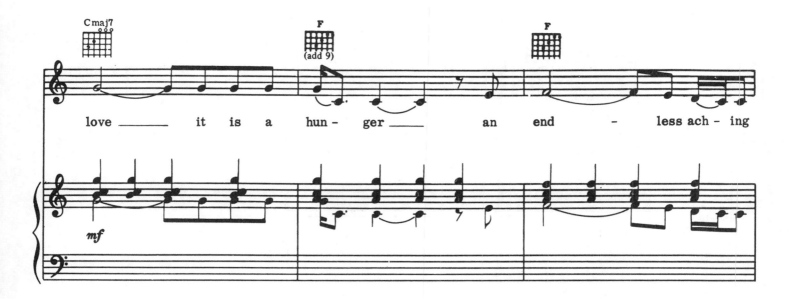

love _____ it is a hun - ger _____ an end - less ach - ing

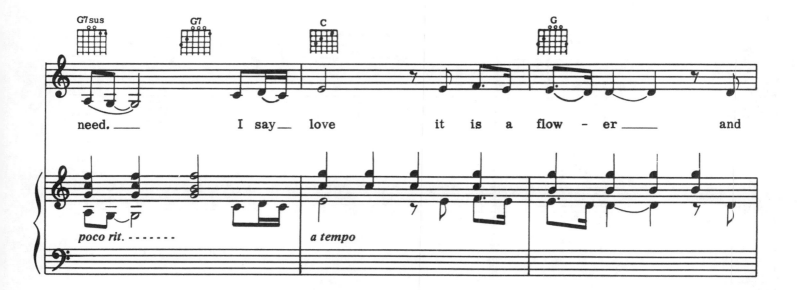

need. _____ I say _ love it is a flow - er _____ and

poco rit. *a tempo*

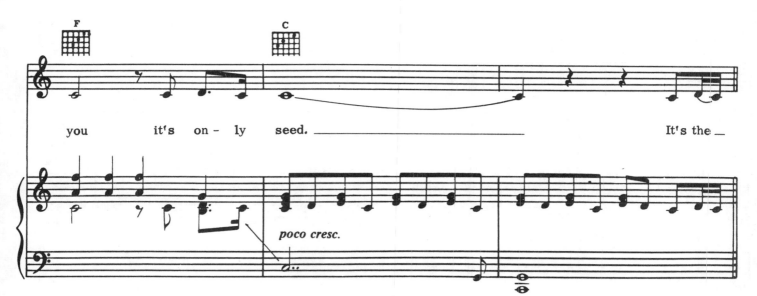

you it's on - ly seed. _____ It's the _

poco cresc.

The Rose - 4 - 2

SONG FROM "M*A*S*H"

(Suicide Is Painless)

Words and Music by
MIKE ALTMAN and JOHNNY MANDEL

Song From "M*A*S*H" - 2 - 1

1. Try to find a way to make
   All our little joys relate
   Without that ever-present hate
   But now I know that it's too late.
       And, Chorus

3. The game of life is hard to play,
   I'm going to lose it anyway,
   The losing card I'll someday lay,
   So this is all I have to say,
       That: Chorus

4. The only way to win, is cheat
   And lay it down before I'm beat,
   And to another give a seat
   For that's the only painless feat.
       'Cause: Chorus

5. The sword of time will pierce our skins,
   It doesn't hurt when it begins
   But as it works it's way on in,
   The pain grows stronger, watch it grin.
       For: Chorus

6. A brave man once requested me
   To answer questions that are key,
   Is it to be or not to be
   And I replied; "Oh, why ask me."
       'Cause: Chorus

SEND IN THE CLOWNS
(From "A Little Night Music")

Music and Lyrics by
STEPHEN SONDHEIM

This arrangement includes Mr. Sondheim's revised lyrics for Barbra Streisand's recording.

SHOW ME THE MEANING
OF BEING LONELY

Words and Music by
MAX MARTIN and HERBERT CRICHLOW

Show Me the Meaning of Being Lonely - 5 - 1

Chorus:

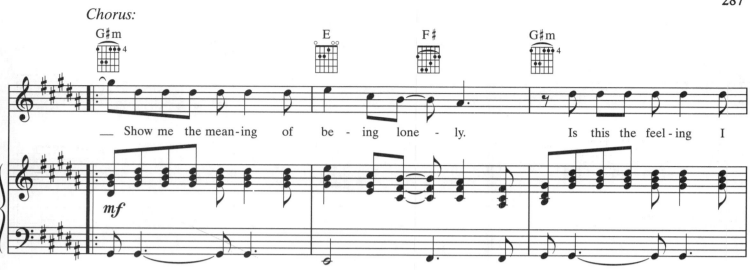

_ Show me the mean-ing of be - ing lone - ly. Is this the feel - ing I

need to walk_ with? Tell me why I can't be there_ where you are._____ There's

1. some-thing miss-ing in my heart. **2.** some-thing miss - ing in my heart.

Show Me the Meaning of Being Lonely - 5 - 5

SMOOTH

Lyrics by
ROB THOMAS

Music and Lyrics by
ITAAL SHUR and ROB THOMAS

Smooth - 5 - 1

same as the e-mo-tion that I get from you.____ You got the kind of lov-ing that can

To Coda |1.

be so smooth,_ yeah. Give me your heart,_ make it real____ or else for-get a-bout it.

|2.

N.C.

D.S. % al Coda

2. Well, I'll tell you ____ or else for-get a-bout it.

Smooth - 5 - 4

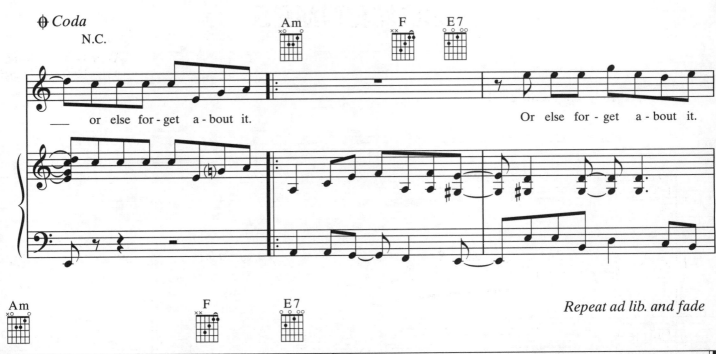

Coda
N.C.

Am   F   E7

or else for - get a - bout it.   Or else for - get a - bout it.

Am   F   E7   *Repeat ad lib. and fade*

Or else for - get a - bout it.

Verse 2:
Well, I'll tell you one thing,
If you would leave, it be a crying shame.
In every breath and every word
I hear your name calling me out, yeah.
Well, out from the barrio,
You hear my rhythm on your radio.
You feel the tugging of the world,
So soft and slow, turning you 'round and 'round.
(To Pre-Chorus:)

SOMETIMES

Words and Music by
JÖRGEN ELOFSSON

Bridge:

PROUD MARY

Words and Music by
JOHN C. FOGERTY

VERSE

Left a good job____ in the ci-ty,____ Work-in' for The Man ev-'ry night and day,____
Cleaned a lot of plates in Mem-phis, Pumped a lot of pain in____ New Or-leans,____

And I nev-er lost one min-ute of sleep-in', Wor-ry-in' 'bout the way things might have been.____
But I nev-er saw the good_side of the ci-ty, Un-til I hitched a ride on a riv-er boat queen.____

CHORUS

Big wheel____ keep on____ turn-in',____ Proud Mar-y keep on burn-in',____ Roll-

From the M-G-M Motion Picture "DOCTOR ZHIVAGO"

SOMEWHERE, MY LOVE
(Lara's Theme from "Doctor Zhivago")

Lyrics by
PAUL FRANCIS JARRE

Music by
MAURICE JARRE

Moderately

Verse: Ad lib.

Where are the beau-ti-ful days? Where are the sleigh-rides 'til dawn?

Where are the ten-der mo-ments of splen-dor? Where have they gone? Where have they gone?

Moderately with expression

Some - where, My Love there will be songs to sing,

Somewhere, My Love - 3 - 1

CAN'T FIGHT THE MOONLIGHT
(Theme from Coyote Ugly)

Words and Music by
DIANE WARREN

Can't Fight the Moonlight - 5 - 1

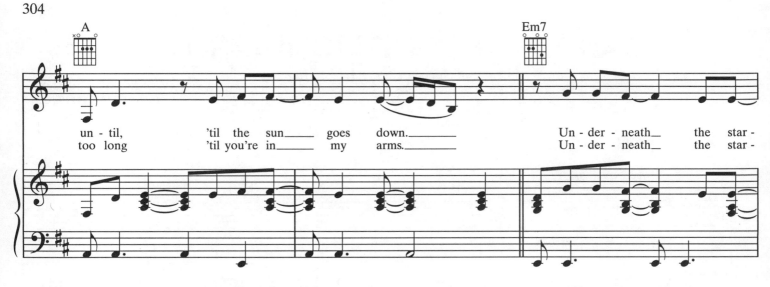

un - til,   'til the sun___ goes down.___   Un - der - neath___ the star-
too long   'til you're in___ my arms.___   Un - der - neath___ the star-

light, star - light,___   there's a mag - i - cal feel - ing so___ right.
light, star - light,___   we'll be lost___ in a rhy - thm so___ right.

Chorus:

It will take__ you in___ to-night. ⎱
Feel it steal__ your heart___ to-night. ⎰   You can try_____ to re - sist,__ try to hide_

___ from my kiss,___ but you know,___ but you know__ that you   can't fight the moon-light. Deep_

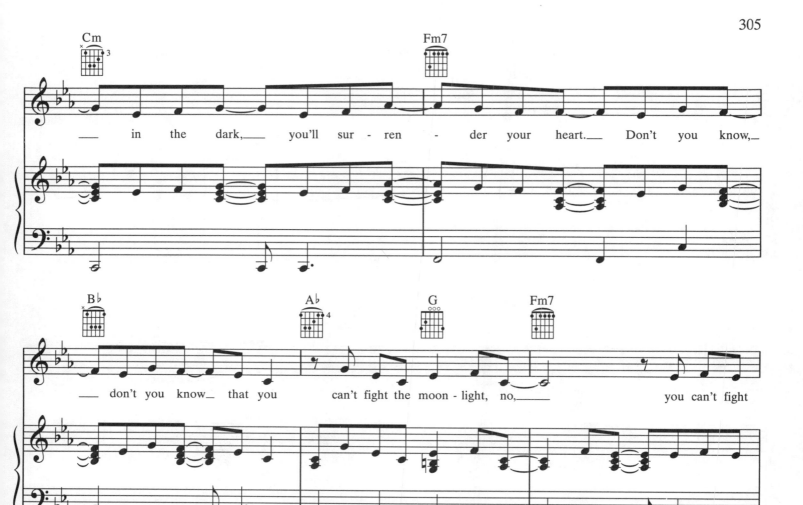

Can't Fight the Moonlight - 5 - 3

Bridge:

Can't fight__ it.__ Don't try__ it, you're__ nev -

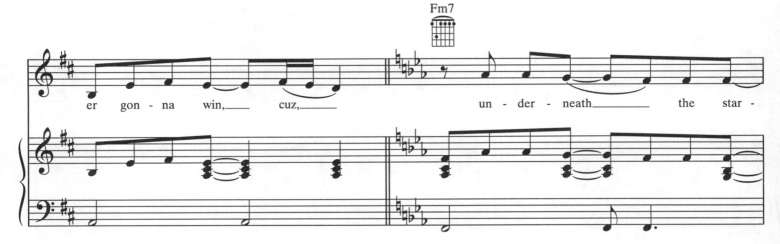

er gon - na win,__ cuz,__ un - der - neath__ the star -

light, star - light,__ there's a mag - i - cal feel - ing so__ right.

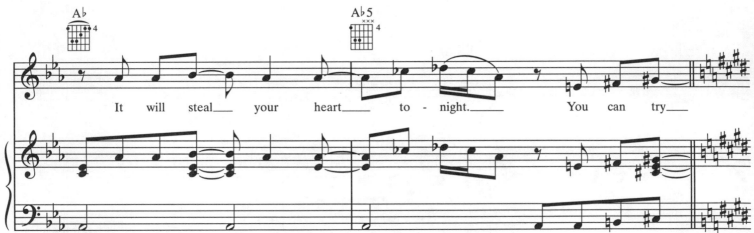

It will steal__ your heart__ to - night.__ You can try__

STAIRWAY TO HEAVEN

Words and Music by
JIMMY PAGE and
ROBERT PLANT

There's a la-dy who's sure —— all that glit-ters is gold__ and she's buy-ing a stair-way —— to

310

316

roll.

And she's buy - ing a stair - way to heav - en.

From the Broadway Musical "FIDDLER ON THE ROOF"

SUNRISE, SUNSET

Lyrics by
SHELDON HARNICK

Music by
JERRY BOCK

Moderately Slow Waltz tempo *(soulful and wistful)*

1. Is this the lit - tle girl I car - ried?
2. Now is the lit - tle boy a bride - groom,

Is this the lit - tle boy at play?
Now is the lit - tle girl a bride.

I don't re -
Un - der the

mem - ber grow - ing old - er,
can - o - py I see them,

When did
Side by

Sunrise, Sunset - 4 - 1

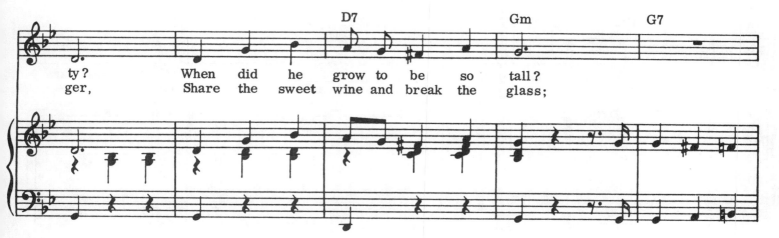

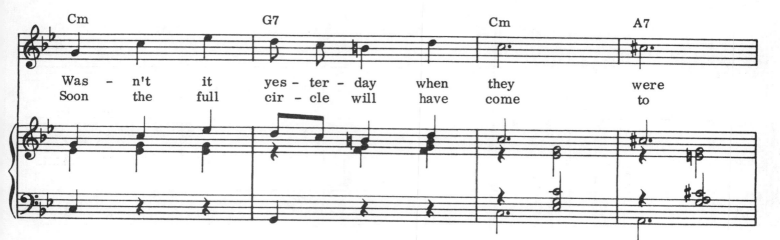

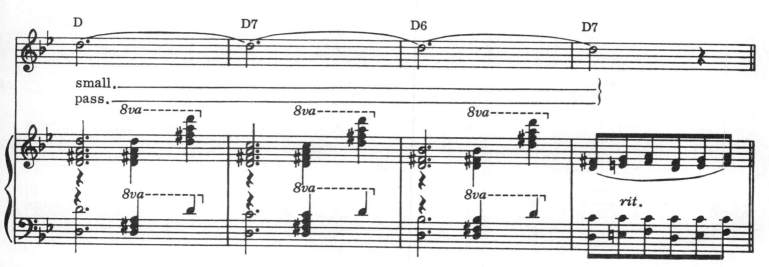

Sunrise, Sunset - 4 - 2

320

Chorus

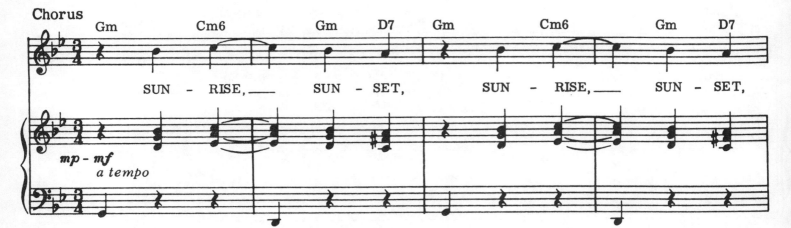

SUN - RISE, ___ SUN - SET, SUN - RISE, ___ SUN - SET,

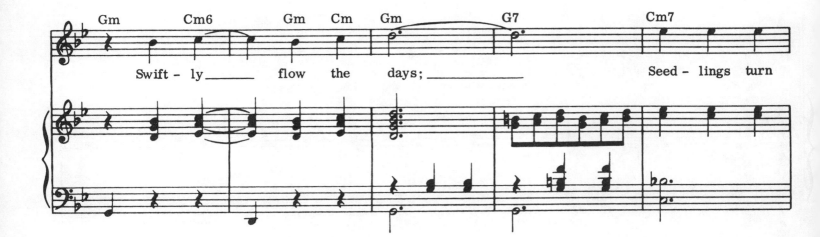

Swift - ly ___ flow the days; _____ Seed - lings turn

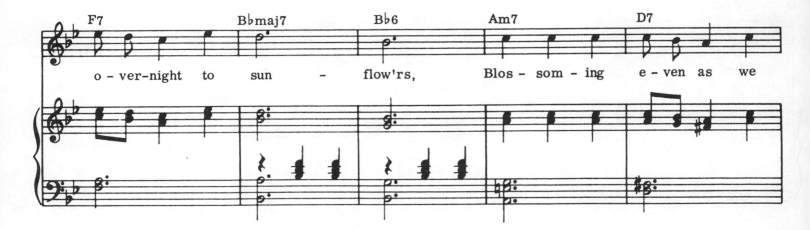

o - ver-night to sun - flow'rs, Blos - som - ing e - ven as we

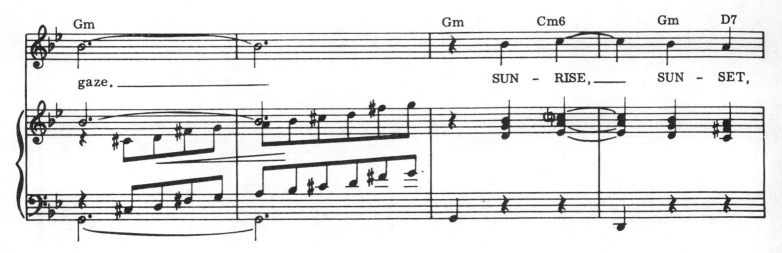

gaze. _____ SUN - RISE, ___ SUN - SET,

Sunrise, Sunset - 4 - 3

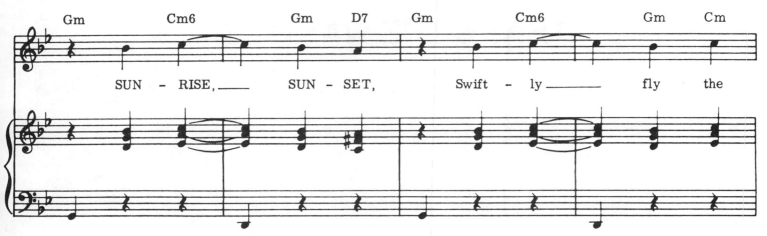

SUN - RISE,_____ SUN - SET, Swift - ly_____ fly the

years;_____ One sea - son fol - low - ing an -

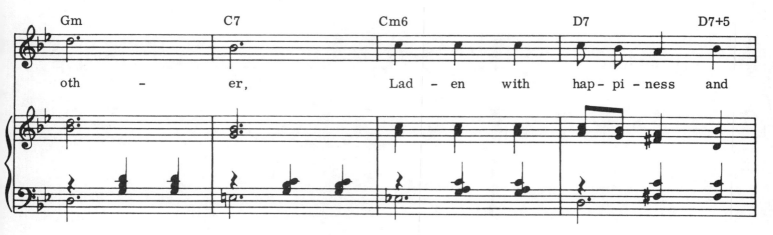

oth - er, Lad - en with hap - pi - ness and

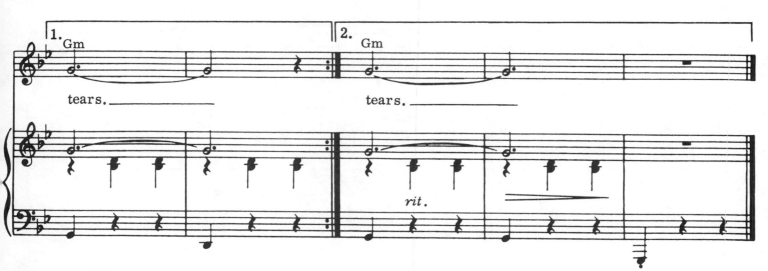

1. tears._____

2. tears._____

rit.

Sunrise, Sunset - 4 - 4

THAT'S THE WAY IT IS

Words and Music by
MAX MARTIN, KRISTIAN LUNDIN
and ANDREAS CARLSSON

Moderately slow ♩ = 96

Verse:

read your__ mind__ and I know your__ sto — ry, I
ques — tion__ me__ for a sim — ple__ an — swer,

Chorus:

When you want it the most,___ there's no eas - y way out.___ When you're

read - y to go_____ and your heart's___ left in doubt,___ don't give

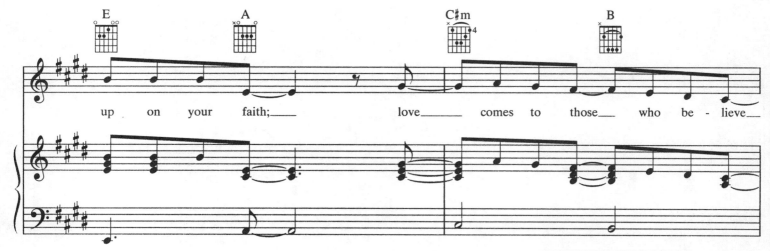

up on your faith;___ love_____ comes to those___ who be - lieve___

1.

___ it,___ and that's the___ way___ it is._____ 2. When you

Chorus:

From the Columbia Motion Picture "ICE CASTLES"

THEME FROM ICE CASTLES
(Through the Eyes of Love)

Lyrics by
CAROLE BAYER SAGER

Music by
MARVIN HAMLISCH

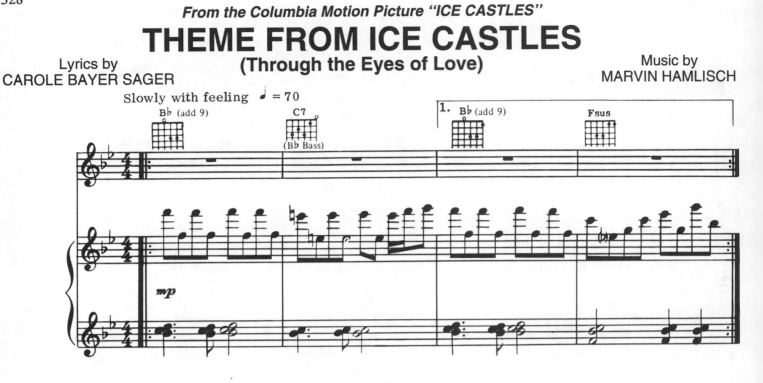

1. Please, don't let this feel - ing
2. now I can take the
3. Please, don't let this feel - ing

end. It's ev-'ry-thing I am, ev-'ry-thing I want to be.
time. I can see my life as it comes up shin - ing now.
end. It might not come a - gain and I want to re - mem - ber

Theme From Ice Castles - 3 - 1

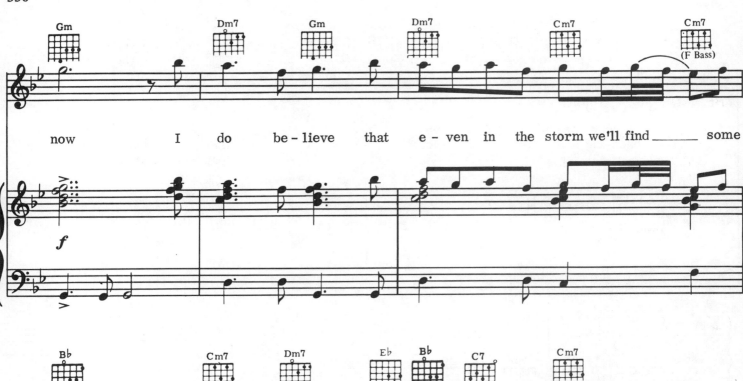

now   I   do   be - lieve   that   e - ven   in   the   storm   we'll   find _____   some

light.   Know - ing you're be - side me I'm all __ right. _____

D.S. al Coda

Coda

through   the   eyes _____   of   love.

From the United Artists Motion Picture "NEW YORK, NEW YORK"

THEME FROM NEW YORK, NEW YORK

Words by
FRED EBB

Music by
JOHN KANDER

Moderately, with rhythm

Theme From New York, New York - 3 - 1

Theme From New York, New York - 3 - 2

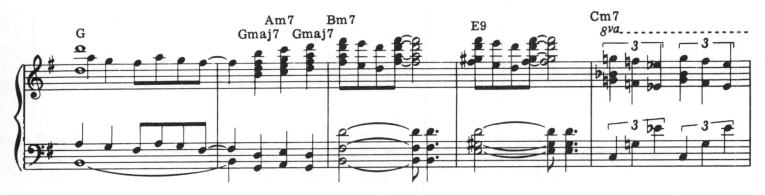

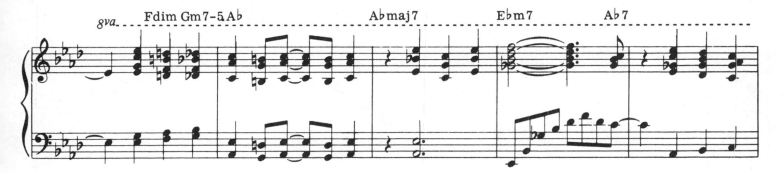

Theme From New York, New York - 3 - 3

THEN THE MORNING COMES

Gtr. tuned down 1/2 step:
⑥ = Eb ③ = Gb
⑤ = Ab ② = Bb
④ = Db ① = Eb

Words and Music by
GREG CAMP

Moderately ♩ = 116

1. Paint the town, take a bow, thank ev-'ry-bod-y.
2. Take your knocks, shake them off, duck ev-'ry-bod-y.

You're gon-na do it a-gain.____ You are the few, the proud,__
You're gon-na take them a-gain.____ You are your foe, your friend,__

Then the Morning Comes - 5 - 1

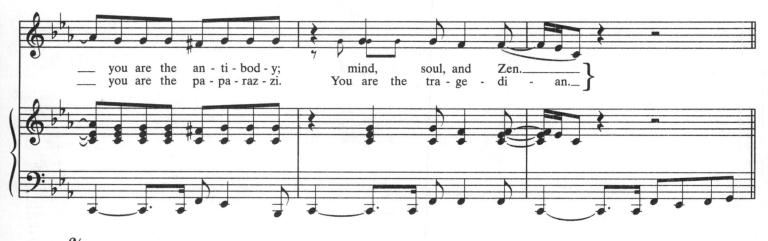

you are the an - ti - bod - y; mind, soul, and Zen.___
you are the pa - pa - raz - zi. You are the tra - ge - di - an.__

And the world's a {1.3. stage.___ / 2. craze.___} And the world's a phase.__ And the end is near._

To Coda ⊕

So push re - wind, just in time, thank an - y - bod - y.

N.C.

You're gon - na do it a - gain. The way that you walk,___

Chorus:

Bridge:

moves so slow,____ kind of like it's say - ing, "I told you so."__

__ Look-ing back be - fore she goes,____ to - mor-row's gon - na

hurt.__

ACROSS THE STARS
(LOVE THEME FROM *STAR WARS* ®: EPISODE II)

Music by
JOHN WILLIAMS

Moderately slow & gently (♩ = 76)

(with pedal)

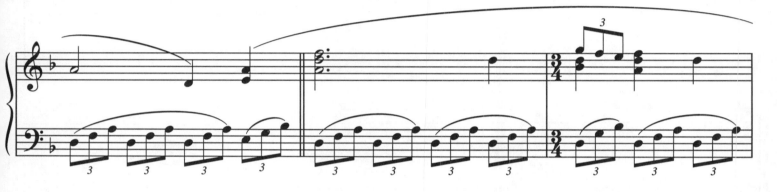

Across the Stars - 5 - 1

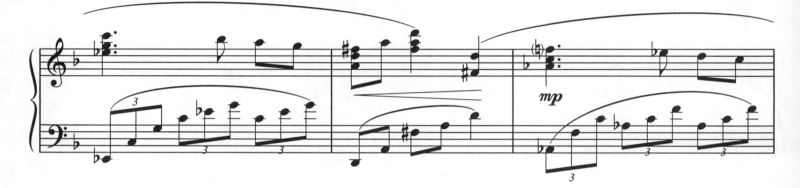

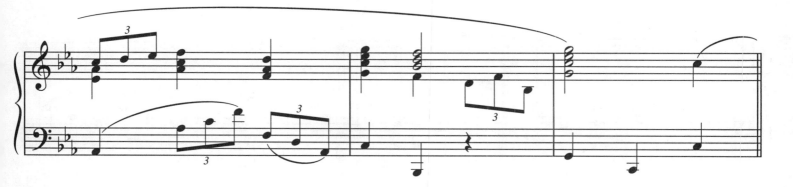

Appassionato

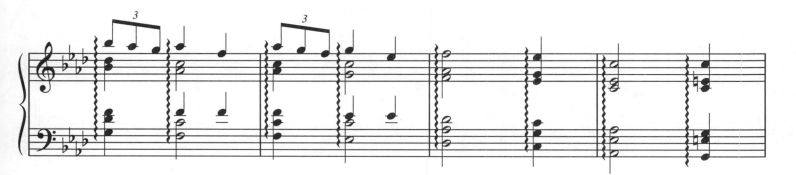

Across the Stars - 5 - 5

I'M ALIVE

Words and Music by
KRISTIAN LUNDIN and ANDREAS CARLSSON

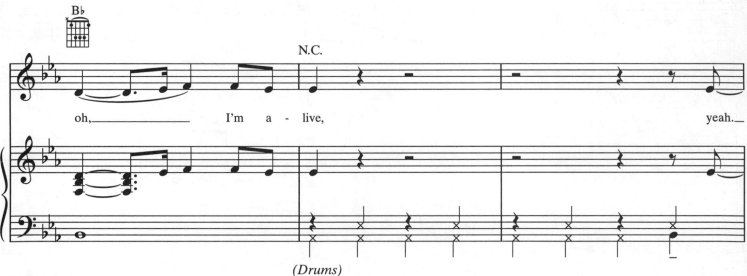

I'm Alive - 7 - 1

347

I'm Alive - 7 - 4

I'm Alive - 7 - 6

UN-BREAK MY HEART

Words and Music by
DIANE WARREN

IF YOU ASKED ME TO

Words and Music by
DIANE WARREN

If You Asked Me To - 4 - 1

YOU NEEDED ME

Words and Music by
RANDY GOODRUM

Slow ballad tempo

1. I cried a tear, you wiped it dry. I was con-
2. (You held my) hand when it was cold. When I was

fused, you cleared my mind. I sold my soul, you bought it
lost, you took me home. You gave me hope, when I was

You Needed Me - 4 - 1

VALENTINE

Composed by
JIM BRICKMAN and JACK KUGELL

Moderately ♩ = 92

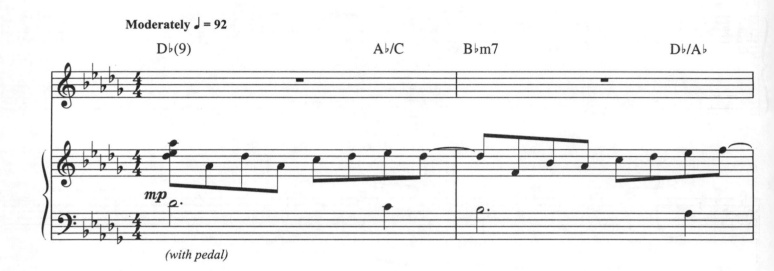

If there were no words,___ no way to speak,___ I

Valentine - 6 - 1

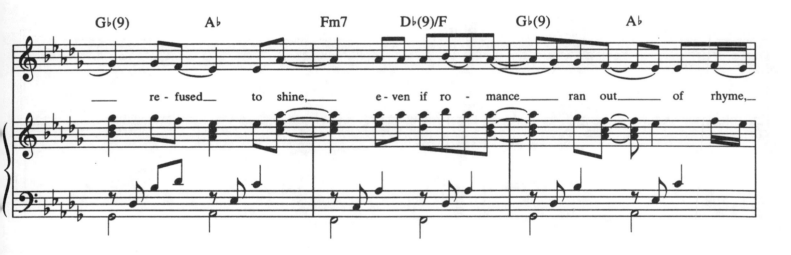

368

Valentine - 6 - 5

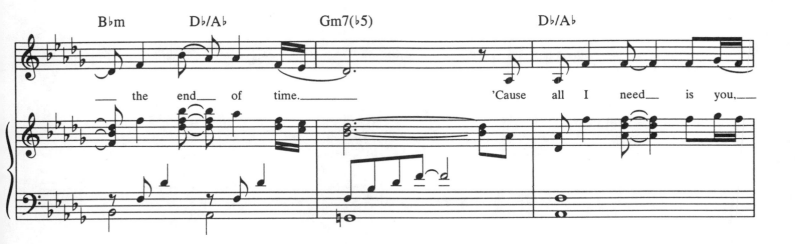

the end of time. 'Cause all I need is you,

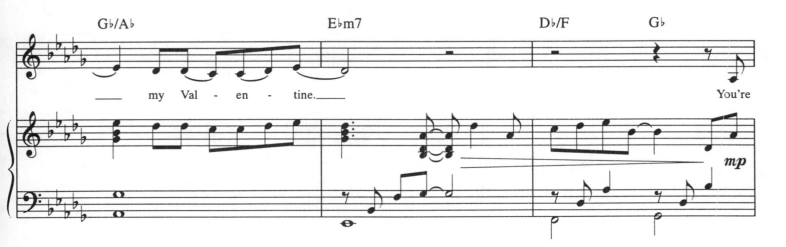

my Val - en - tine. You're

all I need, my love, my Val - en - tine.

WE ARE THE WORLD

Words and Music by
MICHAEL JACKSON and LIONEL RICHIE

We Are the World - 6 - 1

We Are the World - 6 - 2

one. We are the world,___ we are the chil - dren, we are the ones___

___ to make a bright- er day,___ so let's___ start giv - ing. There's a

choice we're mak - ing,_____ we're sav - ing our___ own lives,___ it's true;

___ we make___ bet -ter days,___ just you___ and me.___ **We are the world,___**

WEDDING SONG
(There Is Love)

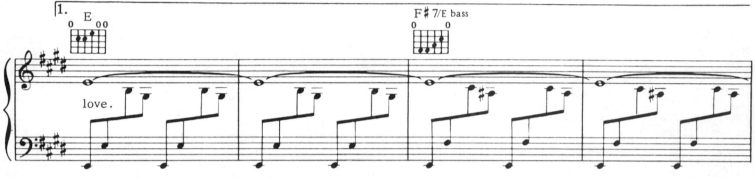

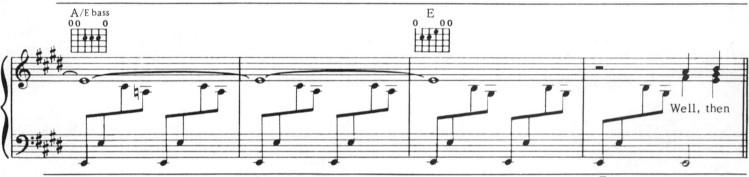

THE WIND BENEATH MY WINGS

Words and Music by
LARRY HENLEY and JEFF SILBAR

It must have been cold there in my shad - ow, ___

to nev - er have sun - light on your

The Wind Beneath My Wings - 7 - 1

The Wind Beneath My Wings - 7 - 3

YOU ARE SO BEAUTIFUL

Words and Music by
BILL PRESTON and BRUCE FISHER

Moderately Slow

You Are So Beau-ti-ful ___ to ___ me.

(Instr. 2nd time)

You Are So Beau-ti-ful ___ to ___

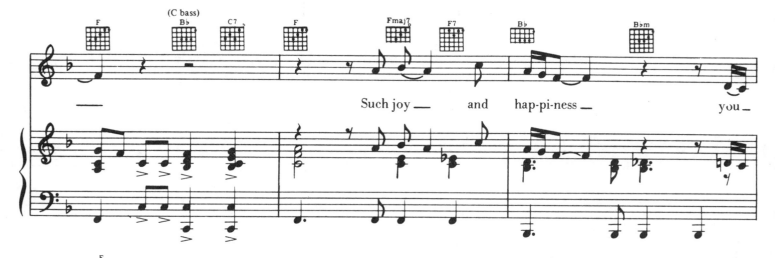

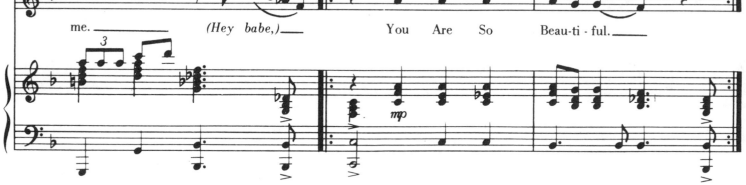

YOU WERE MEANT FOR ME

Words and Music by
JEWEL KILCHER and STEVE POLTZ

Moderate swing feel ♩ = 108

% *Verse:*

1. I hear the clock, it's six A. M.,_____
2.3. *See additional lyrics*

I feel so far____ from where I've been.____ I've got my eggs and my

You Were Meant for Me - 5 - 1

You Were Meant for Me - 5 - 2

Verse 2:

I called my mama, she was out for a walk.
Consoled a cup of coffee, but it didn't wanna talk.
So I picked up a paper, it was more bad news,
More hearts being broken or people being used.
Put on my coat in the pouring rain.
I saw a movie, it just wasn't the same,
'Cause it was happy and I was sad,
And it made me miss you, oh, so bad.
(To Chorus:)

Verse 3:

I brush my teeth and put the cap back on,
I know you hate it when I leave the light on.
I pick a book up and then I turn the sheets down,
And then I take a breath and a good look around.
Put on my pj's and hop into bed.
I'm half alive but I feel mostly dead.
I try and tell myself it'll be all right,
I just shouldn't think anymore tonight.
(To Chorus:)

Recorded by Shania Twain

YOU'RE STILL THE ONE

Words and Music by
SHANIA TWAIN and R.J. LANGE

You're Still the One - 3 - 1

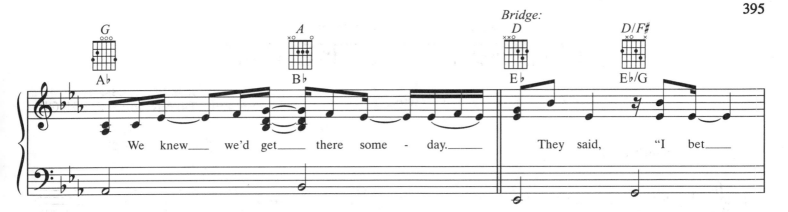

We knew___ we'd get___ there some - day.___ They said, "I bet___

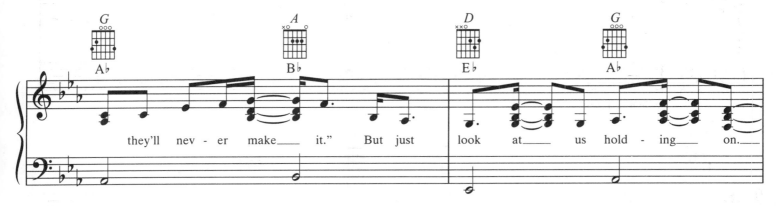

they'll nev - er make___ it." But just look at___ us hold - ing___ on.___

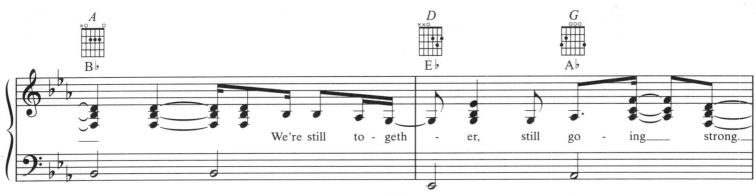

We're still to - geth - er, still go - ing___ strong.

(You're still the one.___) You're still the one I run___ to,

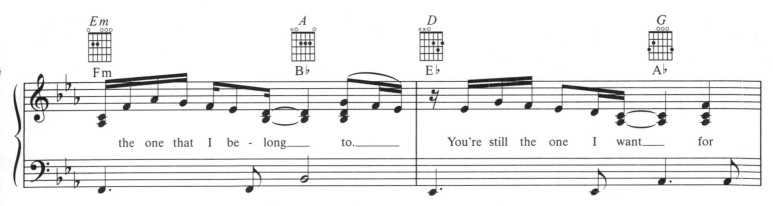

the one that I be - long___ to.___ You're still the one I want___ for

Verse 2:
Ain't nothin' better,
We beat the odds together.
I'm glad we didn't listen.
Look at what we would be missin'.
(To Bridge:)